Women
In The BIBLE

A DEVOTIONAL STUDY OF 50 WOMEN

Women
In The BIBLE

A DEVOTIONAL STUDY OF 50 WOMEN

EUNICE FAITH PRIDDY

Association of Baptists for World Evangelism
P.O. Box 8585
Harrisburg, PA 17105–8585
(717) 774–7000
abwe@abwe.org

ABWE Canada
160 Adelaide St. South, Suite 205
London, Ontario N5Z 3L1
(519) 690–1009
office@abwecanada.org

 PUBLISHING®

DEDICATION

This book is dedicated to my mother, Faith Dark,
a living example of a godly woman.

WOMEN IN THE BIBLE
Copyright © 2001 by ABWE Publishing
Harrisburg, Pennsylvania 17105
Original copyright held by Bible Basics International 1986

Expanded Revised Edition: June 1992
Third Printing Nov. 1994

Library of Congress Cataloging-in Publications Data

Priddy, Eunice Faith, 1952–
  Women In The Bible
  Devotional, Non-fiction
  ISBN 1-888796-23-5 (Trade Paper)

All Scripture quotations are from the King James Version of the Bible.

Printed in the United States of America

TABLE OF CONTENTS

1 THE GODLY WOMAN: *Proverbs 31* 1

2 EVE: *Mother of all Living* 7

3 SARAH: *Mother of Nations: Part 1* 13

4 SARAH: *Mother of Nations: Part 2* 19

5 HAGAR: *A Victim of Circumstances* 25

6 LOT'S WIFE: *Remember Her* 31

7 REBEKAH: *A Manipulating Woman* 37

8 LEAH: *A Loyal Wife* 43

9 DINAH: *Attracted by the World* 49

10 MIRIAM: *Jealousy Brings Judgment* 55

11 PHARAOH'S DAUGHTER: *Simply Used of God* 61

12 RAHAB: *The Changed Harlot* 65

13 ACHSAH: *A Wise Bride* 69

14 DEBORAH: *A Leader Blessed of God* 75

15 DELILAH: *She Betrayed for Money* 81

16 NAOMI: *A Wise Mother-In-Law* 87

17 RUTH: *A Woman Who Chose Wisely: Part 1* 93

18 RUTH: *A Woman Who Chose Wisely: Part 2* 99

19 HANNAH: *A Praying Woman* 105

20 MICHAL: *David's First Wife* 111

21 ABIGAIL: *A Woman of Peace* 117

22 BATHSHEBA: *Mother of King Solomon* 123

23 TWO HARLOT MOTHERS: *Revealing the True Mother's Love* 129

24 THE QUEEN OF SHEBA: *She Searched for Wisdom* 135

25 JEZEBEL: *A Wicked Queen* 141

26 THE WIDOW FROM ZAREPHATH: *A Woman Given to Hospitality* 147

27 THE WIDOW WHOSE OIL MULTIPLIED: *A Woman Who Paid Her Debts* 153

28 THE SHUNAMMITE WOMAN: *A Generous Hostess* 159

29 THE SLAVE GIRL IN NAAMAN'S HOUSE: *A Woman Who Reacted Quickly* 165

30 JEHOSHEBA: *A Woman Who Showed Courage Under Pressure* 169

31 HULDAH: *A Woman Who Spoke the Truth* 175

32 ESTHER: *A Beautiful, Courageous Queen: Part 1* 181

33 ESTHER: *A Beautiful, Courageous Queen: Part 2* 187

34 JOB'S WIFE: *A Woman Who Watched Her Husband Suffer* 193

35 MARY: *Mother of Jesus: Part 1* 199

36 MARY: *Mother of Jesus: Part 2* 205

37 ELIZABETH: *A Woman Blameless Before God* 211

38 ANNA: *A Widow Who Served God* 217

39 SALOME: *A Woman Who Prayed for Her Sons* 221

40 A WOMAN WITH AN ISSUE OF BLOOD: *She Met the Great Physician* 227

41 SYROPHOENICIAN WOMAN: *She Showed Great Faith* 233

42 AN UNNAMED WOMAN: *Known as a "Sinner"* 239

43 MARTHA: *A Woman Given to Hospitality* 245

44 MARY: *She Did What She Could* 251

45 THE SAMARITAN WOMAN: *A Woman with a Powerful Testimony* 257

46 A WOMAN TAKEN IN ADULTERY: *An Unusual Meeting with Jesus* 261

47 MARY MAGDALENE: *Understood True Forgiveness* 267

48 SAPPHIRA: *A Deceitful Woman* 271

49 DORCAS: *A Generous Helper* 277

50 RHODA: *A Persistent Maid* 283

51 LYDIA: *A Businesswoman Who Served* 289

52 PRISCILLA: *United In Ministry with Her Husband* 295

53 EUNICE: *A Woman Who Trained Her Son* 301

54 THE GODLY WOMAN: *Proverbs 31* 305

Bibliography 311

Alphabetical Index 313

Chronological Index 315

ACKNOWLEDGMENTS

My sincere thanks to the Bible Basics International staff who made many valuable suggestions, giving hours of time and effort to the editing and proofreading on the original radio script texts. Marvelia Gonzales Jackson did the Spanish translation and recording for broadcast. Rev. Samuel Montoya and his wife, Imna, were responsible for the final editing and production of the programs in both Spanish and English.

Words are hard to find to express my thanks and pride for my father, Rev. Harold Dark. In his retirement, he used the printing press in his basement for the Lord. Three times he personally printed the original collection of radio scripts into book form.

The constant, continuing love, support, and encouragement given to me by my husband, Glenn, have been what kept me from giving up many times. From the bottom of my heart I thank him for his gentle persistence. His computer skills have also been a tremendous practical help.

Finally, my thanks to the ABWE Publications Director, Jeannie Lockerbie Stephenson, for her guidance and help in making the original radio scripts into a Bible study book. Sincere appreciation to both Jeannie and Kristen Stagg for their hours of editing, which have made this book a reality.

PREFACE

In 1985, the Lord burdened my heart with the need to let women in Third World countries know God values them as individuals. I grew up in Central Africa where women were bought and sold like pieces of property.

Soon after my husband, Glenn, and I were married, we sat week after week reading letters from radio listeners to the Trans World Radio Monte Carlo broadcasts. It became more and more evident to me that women in Muslim, Buddhist, and communist countries also struggled with understanding their importance to God.

With that burden, I began writing a series of radio program scripts for these women. I prayerfully sought guidance from the Lord as I chose the women in the Bible whose lives taught by example, both good and bad.

Knowing the lessons would be translated and used as radio programs, I kept them short, limited the vocabulary, and used cross-cultural illustrations. Often a picture of a certain woman I knew in my childhood came to mind as I wrote the lessons.

Immediately after I had finished writing a few studies, they were translated into Spanish and broadcast over Trans World Radio Bonaire to all of South America. Within the first month of broadcasting, I was thrilled to read a letter from a lady in Venezuela. She said, "I always wondered down deep in my heart if God cared about women. Now after listening to your program I can know that He does. I am glad God loves me, even if I am a woman." WOW! My deepest desire had been completely satisfied in this one letter.

I trust these simple devotional character studies called *Women In The Bible* will be a blessing to you. May the Lord continue to use His Word in the lives of women worldwide, whether it be through radio broadcasts or a Bible study book such as this.

Eunice Priddy

CHAPTER I

THE GODLY WOMAN

PROVERBS 31

Have you ever taken the time to go through the Bible and count the number of women named? Someone did, and found over 150 women, godly and ungodly, who can teach us valuable life lessons. Isn't God good to give us so many examples to learn from?

The Godly Woman of Proverbs 31

Before we study some of the individual women named in the Bible, we will look at the unnamed, godly woman described in Proverbs 31. This woman is certainly an example of success. She knew and recognized her skills, and she used them with joy. The secret of her success was her relationship with God.

The godly woman in Proverbs 31 was used to do great things for God because she trusted in Him. Many of us women think of ourselves as inferior. We need to remember God uses anyone—man or woman—who is obedient to Him and who trusts in Him. God does not use any of us because we are "superhuman," or because we do the impossible. Rather, God uses us when, in dependence on Him, we do our best with the abilities He gave us.

The words in Proverbs 31 were written by King Lemuel. He gives the advice his own mother gave him. Perhaps this is why we often turn to this passage when we think of mothers. Each of us has a mother. Some may have godly mothers; others have ungodly mothers. Still others of us can't remember our mothers.

We may never have seen her. It doesn't really matter whether we are married, single, widowed, or divorced, or who our mother may have been. We can learn much from these verses of Scripture if we will study them asking God to give us an understanding and obedient heart. Proverbs 31:10–31 says:

> [10] Who can find a virtuous woman? for her price is far above rubies.
>
> [11] The heart of her husband doth safely trust in her, so that he shall have no need of spoil.
>
> [12] She will do him good and not evil all the days of her life.
>
> [13] She seeketh wool, and flax, and worketh willingly with her hands.
>
> [14] She is like the merchants' ships; she bringeth her food from afar.
>
> [15] She riseth also while it is yet night, and giveth meat to her household, and a portion to her maidens.
>
> [16] She considereth a field, and buyeth it: with the fruit of her hands she planteth a vineyard.
>
> [17] She girdeth her loins with strength, and strengtheneth her arms.
>
> [18] She perceiveth that her merchandise is good: her candle goeth not out by night.
>
> [19] She layeth her hands to the spindle, and her hands hold the distaff.
>
> [20] She stretcheth out her hand to the poor; yea, she reacheth forth her hands to the needy.
>
> [21] She is not afraid of the snow for her household: for all her household are clothed with scarlet.
>
> [22] She maketh herself coverings of tapestry; her clothing is silk and purple.
>
> [23] Her husband is known in the gates, when he sitteth among the elders of the land.

²⁴ She maketh fine linen, and selleth it; and delivereth girdles unto the merchant.

²⁵ Strength and honour are her clothing; and she shall rejoice in time to come.

²⁶ She openeth her mouth with wisdom; and in her tongue is the law of kindness.

²⁷ She looketh well to the ways of her household, and eateth not the bread of idleness.

²⁸ Her children arise up, and call her blessed; her husband also, and he praiseth her.

²⁹ Many daughters have done virtuously, but thou excellest them all.

³⁰ Favor is deceitful, and beauty is vain: but a woman that feareth the Lord, she shall be praised.

³¹ Give her of the fruit of her hands; and let her own works praise her in the gates.

She Is Trustworthy

The first thing we notice is that her husband completely trusts her. She is good to him, and he can trust her because she will never do evil to him as long as she lives. As a married woman, is this true in your life? As a mother, do you set this kind of example for your daughters?

She Is Not Lazy

She works willingly with her hands. That reflects her attitude. Are we willing to spend the time it takes to do what is best for our household? Do we try to make sure we have done everything we can? The example of a merchant's ship is used because, like a woman's work, the work aboard a ship at sea is not easy. Let us ask God to help us with our attitude toward work.

She Is a Responsible Woman

The woman of Proverbs 31 was not only a homemaker, she was also a businesswoman. Imagine considering the value of a field, and then actually buying it. Some people in today's society would like us to believe that Christian women must give up all rights if we obey God. This is not true. Living in complete obedience to God gives women more freedom and responsibility. Not only must we look after our households, we may also be employers with the responsibility of caring for those who work for us.

She Is a Woman of Strength and Security

Other qualities mentioned in the verses are the woman's planning abilities, her physical vitality, her various skills, and her attitude toward old age and the future. In addition to all that, she was a good communicator. Families have many needs that only a strong woman in the Lord can fulfill. Read Proverbs 31 again and find each of these qualities of strength and security for yourself.

She Is a Woman of Great Sensitivity

A strong, godly woman must be sensitive, which means having the ability to understand quickly the needs of people around her. We need to ask God to help us learn how to realize when someone is hurting or longing for time by herself or wishes someone would just listen to her. We can all learn how to be more aware of the heart cry of people around us.

Don't be fooled by people who say sensitivity is a weakness. There is great strength and wisdom in God-given sensitivity. How many times have you been helped by someone who was understanding just when you needed it most?

She Is Praiseworthy

Proverbs 31:10 asks the question: "Who can find a virtuous woman?" Another way to say that might be: "Who can find a woman worth noticing?" Who noticed this woman? Her family! Often we women seek praise and attention elsewhere. We try to please anyone and everyone except our own family. They know us too well. But it is in this most intimate of settings—the family—that the godly woman finds her praise.

She Respects the Lord

One more thing stands out as we conclude this study. Her real worth and beauty come alive because she respects the Lord. We all need a sense of worth and beauty. No matter how much we try to improve our outer appearance, our real beauty must come from inside—from the heart. When a woman's heart is right with the Lord, this attitude shows on her face. Psalm 128: 1-2 describes the source of inner beauty and peace: *Blessed is everyone that feareth the Lord; that walketh in his ways. For thou shalt eat the labour of thine hands: happy shalt thou be and it shall be well with thee.*

CLOSING THOUGHTS

Let us ask God to help us be godly women, not only for our friends' or neighbors' sake, but for the sake of our families. Then they, too, will rise up and call us blessed.

FOR DISCUSSION

1. In your own words, explain the meaning of Psalm 128:1–2.
2. Who wrote Proverbs 31?
3. List five characteristics of a godly wife as seen in this passage.
4. Which two family members are listed as praising the godly wife?
5. Name one area in your life where you need to ask God to help you fit the description of a godly woman.

CHAPTER 2

EVE

MOTHER OF ALL LIVING

What must it have been like to be the first woman on Earth? What were her first thoughts when she saw Adam, her husband? Exploring the whole garden of Eden and learning about all the different animals and plants must have been great fun. Let your imagination go for a while and try to picture all of the learning Eve had to do right away.

Creation of Eve

"Woman" is first described in the Bible in Genesis 1:27, where we read God created both man and woman: *"So God created man in his own image, in the image of God created he him; male and female created he them."*

Genesis 2:20–23 continues:

> ²⁰ And Adam gave names to all cattle, and to the fowl of the air, and to every beast of the field; but for Adam there was not found a help meet for him.
> ²¹ And the Lord God caused a deep sleep to fall upon Adam, and he slept: and he took one of his ribs, and he closed up the flesh instead thereof;
> ²² And the rib, which the Lord God had taken from man, made he a woman, and brought her unto man.
> ²³ And Adam said, "This is now bone of my bones, and flesh of my flesh: she shall be called Woman, because she was taken out of Man."

God describes the creation of woman in detail. First, the woman was completely human. We women forget that sometimes. We often expect ourselves to be superhuman as we desperately try to meet all the expectations around us. We think we are expected to be a perfect wife, the star employee at work, the model homemaker always keeping a clinically clean home, a proud mother whose kids are always well behaved, the world's best cook and seamstress. In reality, however, we need to learn to accept ourselves the way God made us and try only to please Him.

Second, woman was created superior to the animal world. Some women consider themselves inferior, less than human. God did not create woman that way. Since some women consider themselves inferior humans, they expect to be treated like dogs, chickens, or to be bought and sold like a cow. They have no concept of their true value before God. All women need to understand fully what God created woman to be and why.

He created women to be man's counterpart—his helper—and since she was made from man himself, she holds an intimate relationship to him.

Eve's Uniqueness

Eve was unique in many ways. She had no other woman to teach her and no one to follow. We women often blame our past and present habits on our childhood. We say, "That's the way I was taught" or "No one ever showed me how to do that." Eve gives us an example of complete dependency on God. She relied on her Creator to teach her how to live, to love, to cope, and to overcome all circumstances without any human example to follow.

Eve was different in that she was never a child, never a daughter, and never a teenager. She could never say to her children, "When I was growing up . . . !" She was the world's first mother. Genesis 5 speaks of the sons and daughters born to Adam and Eve. Verse 4 says: *"And the days of Adam after he had begotten*

Seth were eight hundred years: and he begat sons and daughters." The
Bible doesn't tell us how many children Adam and Eve had. But,
if Eve lived as long as Adam—930 years—there must have been
a lot of children in the world's first family.

Women, we don't need to be discouraged, no matter what
the situation. Eve faced problems similar to ours. God, the Source
of her strength, has not changed. As He helped Eve, He will
help us.

Eve may well have been the most beautiful woman the world
has ever known. She was perfect, complete, and created by God's
own hand. She had no artificial beauty. God does not give us a
description of Eve's physical appearance, but we also don't read
that Adam had any complaints!

Eve's Sin and Its Results

Eve was the first and only woman who started life without a
sin nature. She was pure and holy, created sinless; yet she was also
the first person to commit a sin. She had a perfect environment,
but this did not keep her from the attacks of Satan. It does us no
good to spend our time wishing our circumstances were better.
Like Eve, we make mistakes when we allow willful independence
to make us disobey God.

Yielding to temptation robs us of our fellowship with God.
It also affects those we love. We can see this in Eve's relationship
to Adam and later to her family. All humans are descendants of
this first family and have been born with a sin nature. Romans
5:12 says, *"Wherefore, as by one man sin entered into the world, and
death by sin; and so death passed upon all men, for that all have
sinned."*

Eve was the world's first fashion designer. She made fig-leaf
aprons! Before sin came into the world, Adam and Eve were
naked and were not ashamed. The Scripture says: *"And the eyes of
them both were opened, and they knew that they were naked. And they
sewed fig leaves together, and made themselves aprons"* (Genesis 3:7).

God rejected their fig-leaf aprons. The Bible gives us no

record of God verbally rebuking them for their leaf clothes. He simply corrected the situation. Genesis 3:21 says: *"Unto Adam also and to his wife did the Lord God make coats of skins, and clothed them."* Later, however, when God gave His laws to the children of Israel, He made it clear that the blood of an animal was required as an offering to pay for sin. Hebrews 9:22 says: *"And almost all things are by the law purged with blood; and without shedding of blood is no remission."*

Why did God reject the fig-leaf clothing? Because it was Adam and Eve's own attempt to cover up their sin. Instead, God provided coats of skin from an animal sacrifice. Thus, clothing is a reminder of sin and its consequences.

Eve's Imperfect Children

The Bible tells us the story of Eve's first two sons, Cain and Abel. Cain was a farmer; Abel was a shepherd. These boys must have brought much joy into Eve's life. It appears Eve faithfully taught her children how to live in order to please God. The Bible tells us that each son offered sacrifices to God.

God refused Cain's sacrifice of the fruit of the Earth. Remember, Eve's first attempt at making clothing was also refused by God. The big difference, however, is that Eve accepted what God had to say, and wore the clothing He made from animal skins. Cain, on the other hand, killed his brother out of anger at God. Imagine the sorrow this must have been for Eve. On top of that sorrow and shame, she had to bury her second son. Surely, no woman could hurt any more than Eve did at that time.

In Eve's time of need, God gave her another son. By naming him Seth, Eve expressed her faith in God's love, mercy, and provision. Genesis 4:25 records this: *"And Adam knew his wife again; and she bare a son, and called his name Seth: For God, said she, hath appointed me another seed instead of Abel, whom Cain slew."* Eve did not become bitter. She trusted in God and moved on in her life.

Eve's Redemption

Eve was the first to sin. She saw the consequences of her sin when she stood at the grave of her murdered son. But Eve was also the first woman to hear God's prophecy of His own Son's death on the Cross when God told the serpent, the devil: *"And I will put enmity between thee and the woman and between thy seed and her seed: it shall bruise thy head, and thou shalt bruise his heel"* (Genesis 3:15).

Through a woman, God's world that was so beautiful became spotted with the ugliness of sin. Also, through a woman, God's Son was born into the world. At the cross, when Jesus cried, *"It is finished,"* He conquered all the powers and satanic forces that Adam and Eve's sin had brought upon mankind. What a wonderful God we have!

CLOSING THOUGHTS

Eve was created to be Adam's helpmate. She was to help Adam fulfill God's mandate to cultivate and care for the earth. Think about your situation. If you are married, are you and your husband working together to fulfill God's plan for your lives?

Eve was tempted by Satan, and sinned. Are you aware of Satan's methods of tempting you today? Are you prepared for these attacks? What thoughts must Eve have had about herself when she and Adam had to leave their beautiful home in the Garden of Eden? If you had been in her place, would you not have had some sense of failure? How do you cope when you sin? It is sobering to realize that you cannot change or stop the consequences of your sin. Eve lived with the impact of her sin in her home. It is important to see, though, that she was not paralyzed by the past. She accepted God's forgiveness and lived in expectation of the promised Savior.

I hope we all have a new appreciation for the life and example God gave us through Eve. As the Bible says, *"Adam called his wife's name Eve; because she was the mother of all living"* (Genesis 3:20).

FOR DISCUSSION

1. What characteristics were uniquely given to woman in her creation?
2. List three ways in which Eve was different from women today.
3. Eve did many things no woman had done before. Name three.
4. What did Eve do which enabled her to live victoriously rather than be defeated by her sin?
5. In what area of your life can you identify with Eve? Why?

CHAPTER 3

SARAH

MOTHER OF NATIONS: PART I

In this lesson and the next, we will look at the life of Sarah, Abraham's wife. Much is said about her both in the Old and New Testaments. She holds an important place in Hebrew history books because she is the mother of the Jewish people.

The life of Sarah vividly shows how holy, righteous, and yet loving God is. He will not be mocked, but He shows true mercy. He hears the prayers of His children and knows the deepest desire of their hearts.

Sarah's Background

When we first meet Sarah, her name is Sarai. God changed both her name and Abram's when He appeared to Abram to establish a covenant with him. Sarai became Sarah, which means princess. Abram became Abraham when God said to him, *"for a father of many nations have I made thee"* (Genesis 17:5b).

In our day, people sometimes change their names for various reasons. Name changes in the Bible, however, have great significance because it is God who makes the changes. In changing Abram and Sarai's names, God gave a seal or sign of His promise to them. We read about this in Genesis 17:3–5 and 17:15–16:

> ³ And Abram fell on his face: and God talked with him, saying,
>
> ⁴ As for me, behold, my covenant is with thee, and thou shalt be a father of many nations.

⁵ Neither shall thy name any more be called Abram, but thy name shall be Abraham; for a father of many nations have I made thee.

¹⁵ And God said unto Abraham, As for Sarai thy wife, thou shalt not call her name Sarai, but Sarah shall her name be.

¹⁶ And I will bless her, and give thee a son also of her: yea, I will bless her, and she shall be a mother of nations; kings of people shall be of her.

Sarah came from a city called Ur, of the Chaldees in the land of Babylonia. She was the daughter of Terah, the father of Abraham. That made her Abraham's half sister. Even though they had the same father, the marriage was acceptable according to local custom because they had different mothers (Genesis 20:12).

Sarah, Mother of Nations

Sarah is unique because she and her husband were the first parents of the great Jewish race, yet they came from an idolatrous culture. Even Terah, their father, served other gods according to Joshua 24:2. At that time, there was no distinction between Jews and Gentiles because the Jewish nation did not yet exist. Abraham was the first man ever to be called a Hebrew (Genesis 14:13). That happened after God promised to make his descendants a great nation: *"Now the Lord had said to Abram, Get thee out of thy country, and from thy kindred, and from thy father's house, unto a land that I will show thee: And I will make of thee a great nation, and I will bless thee and make thy name great; and thou shalt be a blessing"* (Genesis 12:2).

Genesis 17:15–16 tells of Sarai's name change: *"And God said unto Abraham, As for Sarai thy wife, thou shalt not call her name Sarai, but Sarah shalt her name be. And I will bless her, and give thee a son also of her: yea, I will bless her, and she shall be a mother of nations."* Hebrew folklore refers to Sarah as the next most perfect woman after Eve, who is known as the "mother of all living." Sarah holds the title "mother of nations." Without doubt, she is one of the most important women in world history.

What made Sarah so important and such an outstanding woman? One key factor was her faith. Hebrews 11:11 says, *"Through faith also Sarah herself received strength to conceive seed, and was delivered of a child when she was past age, because she judged him faithful who had promised."*

Did you notice the secret? Sarah knew God would be faithful to His promise. This is an important lesson for all of us to learn. If we trust in or rely on anything less than God, who is perfect, we ourselves become less than God wants us to be. Often we fail in our Christian lives because we trust in our own abilities rather than God's. Sarah's view of God is the first important lesson we learn from her.

God Calls Abraham

We cannot study Sarah without considering Abraham because they were husband and wife. They were living in Haran when God came to Abraham one day and told him He wanted them to move. Not only did He want them to move, but He wanted them to go in total faith. God did not tell them where they were moving, God told them to go to a land that He would show them (Genesis 12:1).

Unfortunately, Abraham only partially obeyed God the first time he was told to move (Genesis 11:31). He did two things he should not have done. First, he took relatives with him when God had not told him to do so. Secondly, Abraham stopped short of the "land that God would show him" when he settled for a while in Haran.

In Genesis 12:1–5 God again appeared to Abraham and told him to move on. The Bible says Abraham went as the Lord had spoken to him. Sarah, of course, went with him. So, for the second time, Sarah has to leave her home, her family, and everything known to her. She followed her husband, as he, by faith, followed the Lord.

Abraham and Sarah were together in this move in obedience to God. The Bible does not tell us of either one complaining or asking God why. Leaving their homeland did not divide their marriage. Neither did it lessen their love for each other.

The Bible also gives no indication that Sarah wanted to go back. Rather, she is praised throughout Scripture for her reverence and obedience to her husband.

Wherever Abraham went, his prosperity increased and he became a very wealthy man. Even riches and position did not divide Abraham and Sarah's commitment to each other. Today many marriages collapse when either the husband or the wife gets a better job or higher education. We can learn from Sarah's commitment to her husband.

Abraham and Sarah's Deception

Famine broke out as Abraham and Sarah traveled in the southern part of the land God had given them, so they decided to go to Egypt. Sarah was a beautiful woman, and Abraham was afraid to tell the king of Egypt she was his wife. He feared the king would kill him and take Sarah into his harem. So the couple devised a plan.

Abraham told the king Sarah was his sister. That was true, but only half the truth. The king did take Sarah into his home and wanted to sleep with her. But God told the king not to touch Sarah because she was another man's wife. God protected both Abraham and Sarah. How much better, though, if they had trusted Him completely, rather than scheming on their own.

CLOSING THOUGHTS

Abraham and Sarah sinned just as we do. The Bible records their failures, and yet God still used them mightily. People often think that if they make one mistake, that's it! God won't use them any more. That is not true. If you have sinned, confess it to God and make amends if needed. God's Word says: *"If we confess our sins, He is faithful and just to forgive us our sins and to cleanse us from all unrighteousness"* (1 John 1:9).

In your situation, too, God can and will forgive your sin, and restore you to a place of joy and service in His kingdom.

FOR DISCUSSION
1. Describe Sarah's background.
2. What special title was given to Sarah?
3. Name two important lessons about God we can learn from Sarah.
4. Name two sins in Abraham and Sarah's lives
5. Does one mistake disqualify a person from God's service forever? Explain your answer.

CHAPTER 4

SARAH

MOTHER OF NATIONS: PART 2

We have looked at Sarah's background, her obedience and loyalty to her husband, and at Abraham and Sarah's deception. This lesson teaches that Sarah's part in the half-truth did not mean the end of her worth. God made a promise to Sarah, and He kept his word.

Sarah's Barrenness

Even though Abraham was a wealthy man and Sarah probably never lacked for anything money could buy, she had a great sadness. The couple shared a long and happy marriage, but they had no children.

God had promised to give them a son and to make them a great nation. But the days turned to months and the months to years. Abraham and Sarah grew older and it became physically impossible for Sarah to have children.

Ten years after God promised them a child, Sarah became desperate and devised another plan. Sometimes we are so slow to learn from past experiences. We saw in the previous chapter how Abraham and Sarah deceived the Egyptians to avoid possible trouble. God lovingly rescued them. Now, once again, Sarah schemed to have children in a way that was not God's plan. Does it surprise you that Abraham went along with Sarah?

But before we are too harsh on Abraham and Sarah, we need to look at our own lives. How often do we try to help God by coming up with our own plans? We need to let God work out

His promises in His own way. That is better than worrying. The sad thing is that some of us would rather worry!

Sarah's plan was to give her maid, Hagar, to Abraham to bear a child. By this means, Sarah would have a child who was Abraham's son. Sarah reasoned that this was a way to fulfill God's promise. The story is found in Genesis 16:1–2, 4, 15–16:

> ¹ Now Sarai Abram's wife bare him no children: and she had an handmaid, an Egyptian, whose name was Hagar.
>
> ² And Sarai said unto Abram, Behold now, the LORD hath restrained me from bearing: I pray thee, go in unto my maid; it may be that I may obtain children by her. And Abram hearkened to the voice of Sarai.
>
> ⁴ And he went in unto Hagar, and she conceived: and when she saw that she had conceived, her mistress was despised in her eyes.
>
> ¹⁵ And Hagar bare Abram a son: and Abram called his son's name, which Hagar bare, Ishmael.
>
> ¹⁶ And Abram was fourscore and six years old, when Hagar bare Ishmael to Abram.

Sarah's scheme was not part of God's plan. God came to Abraham and Sarah again. He changed their names and repeated His promise to give them a child. God specifically said that He would give Abraham a son through Sarah. At the right time, God fulfilled His promise, as we read in Genesis 21:1–5:

> ¹ And the LORD visited Sarah as he had said, and the LORD did unto Sarah as he had spoken.
>
> ² For Sarah conceived, and bare Abraham a son in his old age, at the set time of which God had spoken to him.
>
> ³ And Abraham called the name of his son that was born unto him, whom Sarah bare to him, Isaac.

⁴ And Abraham circumcised his son Isaac being eight days old, as God had commanded him.

⁵ And Abraham was an hundred years old, when his son Isaac was born unto him.

The Jewish people, God's chosen nation, were brought into being through the miraculous birth of Isaac.

What happened to Sarah after Isaac was born? The Bible doesn't give a lot of detail, but it does tell us about one event in Genesis 21. Abraham gave a great feast to celebrate Isaac's weaning. At the feast, Ishmael, Abraham's son by Hagar, mocked Isaac. Sarah went to Abraham and asked him to send Hagar and Ishmael away. Abraham was greatly troubled, but God spoke to him as we read in Genesis 21:12–13:

¹² And God said unto Abraham, Let it not be grievous in thy sight because of the lad, and because of thy bondwoman; in all that Sarah hath said unto thee, hearken unto her voice; for in Isaac shall thy seed be called.

¹³ And also of the son of the bondwoman will I make a nation, because he is thy seed.

God didn't usually tell a husband to do as his wife instructed. Even in this case, Abraham sent Ishmael away because God told him to, not because Sarah told him to. Wives certainly can share their ideas and feelings with their husbands, but as head of the house, the husband is the one to make decisions based on what God wants him to do.

Sarah's Death

The Bible says Sarah died at the age of 127. She is the only woman whose age at death is stated in Scripture. Abraham lived another 38 years after Sarah died. In Genesis 15:15, the Lord promised Abraham a "good old age." This in itself was a significant proof of the faithfulness of God. Godliness is often connected with longevity.

Sarah and Abraham had lived for many years as nomads. However, when Sarah died, Abraham bought a piece of property in which to bury her, rather than placing her body somewhere that could be easily forgotten. Abraham purchased a cave at Machpelah and buried Sarah there.

We are told in Genesis 25 that when Abraham died at the age of 175, his sons buried him next to Sarah in the same cave. Even in death, we see them side by side after their long and eventful life together.

Sarah Used as an Example by New Testament Writers

In Galatians 4:21–31, Paul uses Hagar and Sarah and their sons as an example to show that law and grace cannot exist together. Hagar's son was the son born in the ordinary way; he represents trying to obtain salvation based on works of the law. Isaac was the son born because of God's promise; he represents salvation obtained by the grace and promise of God. Paul draws the contrast between law and grace. The law binds us to our own limits but grace frees us, making room for God to work.

The apostle Peter also uses Sarah as an example of obedience and submission of a married woman to her husband. In 1 Peter 3:5–6 he wrote: *"For in this way in former times the holy women also, who hoped in God, used to adorn themselves, being submissive to their own husbands: Even as Sarah obeyed Abraham . . ."*

The dictionary defines submission as "the act of yielding oneself to the authority or will of another." As married women, we are willingly to accept and follow the leadership and authority of our husbands just as we accept and follow the leadership of the Lord. Many women object to the Bible's teaching about submission. Some feel they become less of a person if they are submissive to their husbands.

Sarah, however, did not lose her identity. She was a beautiful woman physically as well as strong willed and determined. Yet nowhere in Scripture do we read of her disobeying her husband.

Some women may find it hard to obey their husbands because the wife is a believer in Jesus Christ and the husband does not worship the true God. There may be situations when obeying a husband would mean going against God's Word. Most often, however, since the Bible uses Sarah as a pattern for women, we would do well to heed her example of submission and obedience.

CLOSING THOUGHTS

If you are married or considering marriage, take a moment to evaluate your relationship to your husband or husband-to-be. Are you willing to follow this command? *"Wives, submit yourselves unto your own husbands, as unto the Lord. For the husband is the head of the wife, even as Christ is the head of the church"* (Ephesians 5:22).

If submission is an area in your life where you need God's help, ask Him to give you the faith you need to rely on His promises no matter what your circumstances may be.

FOR DISCUSSION

1. Why do you think Sarah thought it necessary to come up with her own plan to have children?
2. In spite of her plan, how did God show mercy to Sarah?
3. Why do you think Abraham agreed with Sarah's plan?
4. What unique event happened at Sarah's death?
5. Discuss how the apostles Paul and Peter used Sarah as an example.

CHAPTER 5

HAGAR

A VICTIM OF CIRCUMSTANCES

Hagar was the servant who bore a son to Abraham at Sarah's request. But this was not God's plan. The resulting jealousy made everyone's life miserable. When Sarah ordered Hagar to go to Abraham, the slave girl did what she was told. Likely, she had no choice in the matter. She was a victim of circumstances.

She is not alone. Many of us have also found ourselves in confused and troubled situations. Sometimes we get into a mess even though we are as innocent as Hagar was. Our troubles may not be the same as Hagar's; nevertheless, the problems are just as real. As we study Hagar's life, I trust we will be encouraged by the great mercy and loving concern God showed to Hagar in her time of need.

Hagar's Background

The Bible does not tell us much about Hagar, who was just a slave. We know nothing of her past or family except that she was an Egyptian servant to Sarah (Genesis 16:1). We can suppose she was the slave girl Abraham bought for his wife, Sarah, while they were in Egypt.

As Hagar's mistress, Sarah was legally entitled to do as she pleased according to the laws of the day. When Sarah could not bear children herself, she gave her servant, Hagar, to her husband to bear children for them. This was a custom consistent with the moral standards of the day.

But that was not God's moral standard. Nor was it His will

for Abraham and Sarah. When Sarah realized Hagar was pregnant, the jealousy began. Sarah complained to her husband, and he told her to do whatever she wanted with Hagar.

Hagar Runs from Sarah

With Abraham's permission, Sarah dealt harshly with Hagar. The slave's situation was so bad that one day Hagar fled into the wilderness. We can read the account from Genesis 16:6–11:

> ⁶ And when Sarai dealt hardly with her, she fled from her face.
>
> ⁷ And the angel of the LORD found her by a fountain of water in the wilderness, by the fountain in the way to Shur.
>
> ⁸ And he said, Hagar, Sarai's maid, whence camest thou? and whither wilt thou go? And she said, I flee from the face of my mistress Sarai.
>
> ⁹ And the angel of the LORD said unto her, Return to thy mistress, and submit thyself under her hands.
>
> ¹⁰ And the angel of the LORD said unto her, I will multiply thy seed exceedingly, that it shall not be numbered for multitude.
>
> ¹¹ And the angel of the LORD said unto her, Behold, thou art with child, and shalt bear a son, and shalt call his name Ishmael; because the LORD hath heard thy affliction.

Running away from Sarah was understandable, but Hagar's actions were not acceptable in God's eyes. The way Sarah treated Hagar was wrong, but two wrongs do not make a right. The angel of the Lord told Hagar to return and be submissive to her mistress. Imagine how hard those words must have been for Hagar to hear.

Reading the rest of the passage, you see that Hagar obeyed what the angel of the Lord told her to do. Maybe, like I do, you wonder how Hagar found the courage to go back. She gained strength to do what was right from God Himself. In Genesis 16:13 Hagar says, *"Thou God seest me."*

Like Hagar, we need to learn to draw strength from God. We gain great comfort, assurance, hope, and strength in knowing—through personal experience—that God has seen us and knows our need no matter what our circumstances are. In the realization that God sees and knows us, our faith can grow. Jesus said, *"Blessed are the pure in heart, for they shall see God"* (Matthew 5:8). Hagar's story is a testimony to this verse.

After her experience with the angel of the Lord in the wilderness, Hagar returned to Sarah and bore Abraham a son whom he named Ishmael. The Bible says Abraham was 86 years old when Ishmael was born and 100 years old when Isaac was born.

This means for 14 years, Sarah had to look at the son of her husband by another woman. It is not too hard to understand the tension this must have caused for everyone: Abraham, Sarah, Hagar, and Ishmael.

Hagar and Ishmael Sent Away

Finally, Isaac was born to Sarah. Then there were even bigger problems! Ishmael mocked Isaac at the party when the little boy was weaned. Sarah reached her limit and could take no more, so she asked Abraham to send Hagar away.

For the second time Hagar found herself in the wilderness. This time she didn't leave by choice; she was sent away, as Genesis 21:14–19 tells us:

> [14] And Abraham rose up early in the morning, and took bread, and a bottle of water, and gave it unto Hagar, putting it on her shoulder, and the child, and sent her away: and she departed, and wandered in the wilderness of Beersheba.
> [15] And the water was spent in the bottle, and she cast the child under one of the shrubs.

¹⁶ And she went, and sat her down over against him a good way off, as it were a bowshot: for she said, Let me not see the death of the child. And she sat over against him, and lift up her voice, and wept.

¹⁷ And God heard the voice of the lad; and the angel of God called to Hagar out of heaven, and said unto her, What aileth thee, Hagar? fear not; for God hath heard the voice of the lad where he is.

¹⁸ Arise, lift up the lad, and hold him in thine hand; for I will make him a great nation.

¹⁹ And God opened her eyes, and she saw a well of water; and she went, and filled the bottle with water, and gave the lad drink.

What a pitiful sight: Hagar and her son dying of thirst! Yet God, in His mercy, did not forget Hagar, who was a victim of circumstances. Nor did He forget Ishmael. Since his mother was an innocent victim, Ishmael certainly was as well—maybe even more so—because he had no choice in his birth. Yet God kept His promise and made a great nation from the descendants of Ishmael—the Arab nations of today.

God's promise to make a great nation from the descendants of Abraham has been fulfilled. Just as you can find people of the Jewish race in almost any country of the world, you also find those from Arab nations. However, the same jealousy and strife seen at the birth of these two nations is clearly evident today in the ongoing Middle East conflict.

Lessons from the Life of Hagar

We can learn much from Hagar's life. First, we learn that we must be on guard against temptations, even when they are forced upon us. In the customs and culture of that time it might have been considered an honor for a slave girl to be given to her owner to bear children. The Bible tells very little of Hagar's background. We do not know if she believed in and worshiped the true God. Therefore, we cannot say if she knew what Sarah ordered her to do was wrong or not. Nor do we know if Hagar could have refused. But that does not change the fact that immorality is a sin before God.

Secondly, Hagar shows us the foolishness of hasty actions. She should not have run away the first time. Whenever we try to take matters into our own control and run ahead of God, we can be sure nothing but trouble lies ahead.

On the positive side, the life account of Hagar reveals the care and concern God shows to the needy and the lowly. Hagar also shows us we can find strength even amidst the hardest trials of life.

Just as we saw in the life of Sarah, Hagar's story reminds us that God is sovereign. He works out His purpose and will according to what He has said.

CLOSING THOUGHTS

I hope this study has been a comfort and help to you, whatever your circumstances. Maybe you don't know God, and wonder how you can talk to Him and tell Him your troubles. The Bible says in Romans 10:13: *"For whosoever shall call upon the name of the Lord shall be saved."*

If you, by faith, ask God to save you, He will hear. He sent His only Son, the Lord Jesus Christ, to die on the Cross for your sins. He also raised Him from the dead on the third day. Surely, with such great love, God will make Himself known to you. Trust Him today!

For believers in Jesus Christ, it is especially hard to trust God when circumstances are beyond our control. We can find the secret of being able to trust God no matter what happens only when we realize God is in control. He knows what is going on in our lives. Nothing takes God by surprise. When we accept what God allows to come into our lives, we can say, like David: *"As for God, his way is perfect"* (Psalm 18:30).

That truth is also confirmed in Romans 8:28: *"And we know that all things work together for good to them that love God, to them who are the called according to his purpose."*

FOR DISCUSSION

1. Why was it wrong for Sarah to give Hagar to Abraham?
2. What character qualities did Hagar show when confronted by the angel of the Lord?
3. Describe the situation in the home between Sarah and Hagar.
4. What consequences still seen today came about as a result of Ishmael's birth?
5. Name two lessons about God we can learn from the life of Hagar.

CHAPTER 6

LOT'S WIFE

REMEMBER HER

God is just. That is why He gives accounts of both good and bad women in His Word. In this lesson we will learn how negative examples can show as effectively as positive ones how we ought to live our lives.

Background on Lot's Wife

As we look at the story of Lot's wife, I pray we will feel the weight of meaning behind one of the shortest verses in the Bible. In Luke 17:32, Jesus said, *"Remember Lot's wife."*

This woman is mentioned twice in the Bible. We do not even know her name. Both Bible references simply refer to her as "Lot's wife." Yet throughout the course of history, she has been remembered as a solemn warning to women everywhere.

Lot was Abraham's nephew. Abraham—originally called Abram—was a rich man who shared his wealth with his nephew. He was also a man who lived righteously before God. As Abraham's and Lot's herds grew and multiplied, arguments developed between their herdsmen, so Abram discussed the problem with Lot. Genesis 13:8–9 says:

> [8] And Abram said unto Lot, Let there be no strife,
> I pray thee, between me and thee, and between my
> herdsmen and thy herdsmen; for we be brethren.
> [9] Is not the whole land before thee? separate thyself,
> I pray thee, from me: if thou wilt take the left hand,

then I will go to the right; or if thou depart to the
right hand, then I will go to the left.

The Bible says Lot looked around and took what he thought
was the best land for his herds. That land lay in the direction of
an evil city called Sodom. Motivated by his selfishness, Lot moved
to Sodom.

Lot's Family

The men of Sodom were wicked and sinned greatly against
the Lord. Lot not only moved in their direction but, before long,
he became a citizen of Sodom. We know he was an honored and
respected man in the community because he sat in the gate, a
place of prominence.

The Bible does not tell us anything more specific about the
background of Lot's wife. But we get the impression she enjoyed
her husband's wealth and position in the city, and she became
attached to material possessions.

The Wickedness of the Sodomites

Continuing the true account of Lot and his family, we read
in Genesis 19:1, 3:

> [1] And there came two angels to Sodom at even; and
> Lot sat in the gate of Sodom: and Lot seeing them rose
> up to meet them; and he bowed himself with his face
> toward the ground;
> [3] . . . and they turned in unto him, and entered into
> his house; and he made them a feast, and did bake
> unleavened bread, and they did eat.

From this text we see that two angels who looked like ordinary men came to visit Lot. He took them home and prepared a
meal for them. We can assume that his wife took part in the food
preparation.

The men of Sodom were so wicked that they wanted to take
the two men out of Lot's house in order to practice their sexual

deviance with them. In his effort to protect his guests, Lot offered his own daughters to satisfy their sexual hunger. This shows how living in Sodom had affected Lot and his family. The Bible goes on to say that just when the men of the city were about to push Lot's door down, the angels performed a miracle, blinding all the men instantly. In their mass confusion, they could not find the door, and Lot's family was safe.

Deliverance by the Grace of God

Genesis 19:12–16 continues the account of the angels' protection of Lot and his family:

> [12] And the men said unto Lot, Hast thou here any besides? son in law, and thy sons, and thy daughters, and whatsoever thou hast in the city, bring them out of this place:
>
> [13] For we will destroy this place, because the cry of them is waxen great before the face of the LORD; and the LORD hath sent us to destroy it.
>
> [14] And Lot went out, and spake unto his sons in law, which married his daughters, and said, Up, get you out of this place; for the LORD will destroy this city. But he seemed as one that mocked unto his sons in law.
>
> [15] And when the morning arose, then the angels hastened Lot, saying, Arise, take thy wife, and thy two daughters, which are here; lest thou be consumed in the iniquity of the city.
>
> [16] And while he lingered, the men laid hold upon his hand, and upon the hand of his wife, and upon the hand of his two daughters; the LORD being merciful unto him: and they brought him forth, and set him without the city.

God, in His kindness, gave all of Lot's family a chance to escape, but many in his family wouldn't listen. Except for his wife and his daughters who were in the house with Lot, the rest of the family were all destroyed, along with the entire city of Sodom.

Remember Lot's Wife

Jesus told us to remember Lot's wife. What should we remember about her? One aspect is the consequence of disobedience. Genesis 19:17, 24–26 explains this:

> [17] And it came to pass, when they had brought them forth abroad, that he said, Escape for thy life; look not behind thee, neither stay thou in all the plain; escape to the mountain, lest thou be consumed.
>
> [24] Then the LORD rained upon Sodom and upon Gomorrah brimstone and fire from the LORD out of heaven;
>
> [25] And he overthrew those cities, and all the plain, and all the inhabitants of the cities, and that which grew upon the ground.
>
> [26] But his wife looked back from behind him, and she became a pillar of salt.

Lot's wife was already well out of Sodom with her husband and two daughters. But what remained behind pulled at her so much, she looked back. She didn't heed the angels' warnings. Her selfish desires and unbelief robbed her of reason, and she paid for her disobedience with her life.

CLOSING THOUGHTS

Certainly the children in Lot's family knew their mother's attitude. They realized she didn't believe what the angels and her husband said would happen. The two youngest daughters actually watched their mother disobey and saw the tragic consequences. Today, too, someone is always watching our actions and our attitudes. How carefully we need to live our lives.

Has God blessed you with material goods, a nice home, a good family, a happy and secure life? Would you be willing to obey God if He asked you to go somewhere or do something for Him if that upset your comfort? Are you willing to give up whatever God asks you to in order to be obedient to Him?

The warning comes to us, too: "Remember Lot's wife."

FOR DISCUSSION

1. In what two places do we find mention of Lot's wife in the Bible?
2. Give two reasons why you think she looked back.
3. What lessons can we learn from her?
4. Name three things that you would have a hard time giving up. Why?
5. What does your family see in your life as being most important to you?

CHAPTER 7

REBEKAH

A MANIPULATING WOMAN

Rebekah's marriage to Isaac can be described as having been "made in heaven." Her story is recorded in Genesis 24. In spite of the beautiful start she and Isaac had, their relationship and home life completely collapsed. Rebekah never learned how to properly manage her household.

We can learn much from Rebekah's life even though she is an example of what *not* to do. Her life had many problems we should try to avoid.

Abraham's Servant Sent

The first part of Rebekah's story tells the way in which she met Isaac, the son God promised to Abraham and Sarah. Abraham left his home country to follow God's leading to the land He promised to Abraham and his descendants. When Sarah died, Abraham refused to bury her among the people of the land, but purchased his own piece of property for a burial place. In the same way, when it was time to find a wife for Isaac, he refused to let his son marry a daughter of the idol worshiping people in the land.

Instead, Abraham sent his most trusted servant to find a wife for his son Isaac. When the servant found Abraham's relatives, he told them his purpose in coming back home. Genesis 24:42–47 explains how the servant met Rebekah and came to Abraham's brother's home:

⁴² And I came this day unto the well, and said, O Lord God of my master Abraham, if now thou do prosper my way which I go:

⁴³ Behold, I stand by the well of water; and it shall come to pass, that when the virgin cometh forth to draw water, and I say to her, Give me, I pray thee, a little water of thy pitcher to drink;

⁴⁴ And she say to me, Both drink thou, and I will also draw for thy camels: let the same be the woman whom the Lord hath appointed out for my master's son.

⁴⁵ And before I had done speaking in mine heart, behold, Rebekah came forth with her pitcher on her shoulder; and she went down unto the well, and drew water: and I said unto her, Let me drink, I pray thee.

⁴⁶ And she made haste, and let down her pitcher from her shoulder, and said, Drink, and I will give thy camels drink also: so I drank, and she made the camels drink also.

⁴⁷ And I asked her, and said, Whose daughter art thou? And she said, the daughter of Bethuel, Nabor's son, whom Milcah bare unto him: and I put the earring upon her face, and the bracelets upon her hands.

The servant immediately recognized God's hand in leading him to Rebekah. She was a relative of Abraham, the exact family he had come to find. He bowed in worship to the Lord God. Rebekah's relatives also recognized God's work and told the servant he could take Rebekah, if she was willing to go. Genesis 24:58 gives her clear answer: *"And they called Rebekah, and said unto her, Wilt thou go with this man? And she said, I will go."*

Rebekah gathered her things, along with the servants given to her, and departed with Abraham's servant to a place she did not know, to become the wife of a man she did not know. Her willingness to follow God was expressed in her answer "I will go."

The question each of us must answer for ourselves is "Am I ready to follow God where He leads when His direction is clear?"

Rebekah and Isaac Meet

Genesis 24:63–67 tells what took place when Isaac and Rebekah met:

> [63] And Isaac went out to meditate in the field at the eventide: and he lifted up his eyes, and saw, and, behold, the camels were coming.
>
> [64] And Rebekah lifted up her eyes, and when she saw Isaac, she lighted off the camel.
>
> [65] For she had said unto the servant, What man is this that walketh in the field to meet us? And the servant had said, It is my master: therefore she took a veil, and covered herself.
>
> [66] And the servant told Isaac all things that he had done.
>
> [67] And Isaac brought her into his mother Sarah's tent, and took Rebekah, and she became his wife; and he loved her: and Isaac was comforted after his mother's death.

Rebekah's Married Life

Rebekah and Isaac loved each other, were married, and enjoyed God's blessing on their lives. But after 20 years of marriage, they still had no children. Isaac prayed for a child, and God answered his prayer by giving them twin boys. Even before the twins were born, Rebekah felt a struggle inside her. She asked the Lord about this. God explained that she was carrying twins. God's prophecy about the twins, given before they were born, is found in Genesis 25:23: *"And the Lord said unto her, Two nations are in thy womb, and two manner of people shall be separated from thy bowels; and the one people shall be stronger than the other people; and the elder shall serve the younger."*

The Bible tells more about the twins in Genesis 25:27–28.

> [27] And the boys grew: and Esau was a cunning hunter, a man of the field; and Jacob was a plain man, dwelling in tents.
> [28] And Isaac loved Esau, because he did eat of his venison: but Rebekah loved Jacob.

As Esau and Jacob grew up, they continued to struggle. One day Esau came home from the fields weak and hungry. Because he was so hungry at that moment, he sold his right of inheritance as Jacob's first-born son for a mere bowl of soup. This gave Jacob a larger share of the inheritance, as well as a greater spiritual blessing.

As Isaac grew old and lost his eyesight, he decided it was time to give his blessing to his oldest son. Rebekah realized what was going to happen. She wanted Jacob, her favorite son, to receive the blessing instead. So, she convinced Jacob to trick his father, and even helped him do it. Jacob received the blessing that Isaac intended for Esau.

When Esau found out what had happened, he was so angry he wanted to kill Jacob. In order to save Jacob's life, Rebekah sent Jacob to her brother Laban's home. Jacob lived and worked there for over 20 years. When he finally returned home, Rebekah had already died. Because of their deception, Rebekah never saw her favorite son again.

Lessons from Rebekah's Life

What happened in Rebekah and Isaac's home? Where did they go wrong? After such a beautiful start, perfectly matched by God, they should have lived happily ever after. What can we learn from Rebekah's life?

First, remember the complete faith in God Rebekah showed when she said to Abraham's servant, "I will go." She was willing to go to an unknown land and to be the bride of an unknown man. Do we have that kind of faith in God?

Rebekah, however, forgot about God's sovereignty. God had told her that the older son would serve the younger one. She should have trusted God and watched Him bring events to pass. Instead, Rebekah took matters into her own hands. It is so easy for us to think we need to help God. We think we can figure out how life should be so that it will be easier for God to work. How foolish we are, yet we do it over and over again.

Another important lesson from Rebekah's life is the harm that favoritism causes in a family. The division caused by favoring one child above another is devastating. We need to examine our own homes and relationships. Often our attitudes toward our children affect our relationships with them and our husband.

CLOSING THOUGHTS

Rebekah was a beautiful woman with many strengths. She was intelligent, courteous, quick thinking, self-motivated, and strong willed. However, she allowed her love for her younger son to turn her into a deceitful woman, betraying her own husband.

Let us not follow Rebekah's bad example; instead, let us allow God to control our personality by His Spirit. We can trust Him to work out His perfect will in our lives and in the lives of our children. Proverbs 14:1 says: *"Every wise woman buildeth her house: but the foolish plucketh it down with her hands."*

Are we building up or tearing down our homes?

FOR DISCUSSION

1. Name two of Rebekah's good qualities that we can try to put into practice in our own lives.
2. Name two of Rebekah's qualities we should try to avoid.
3. If you have children (or teach children), name three spiritual goals you have set for the children in your care.

4. What are you doing to make sure these goals are accomplished?
5. Describe what happened to turn Rebekah's marriage from good to bad.

CHAPTER 8

LEAH

A LOYAL WIFE

Have you ever found yourself in a situation where you are an innocent victim of circumstances? You did not try to get into this situation; it was not even your fault, but there you are! In this chapter, we will look at the life of Leah, a woman who found herself in such a state.

Leah's Background

Leah was the elder daughter of Laban, a sheep farmer living in Haran. Her father tricked Jacob, the man who loved her younger sister, Rachel. Laban gave him Leah on the wedding night instead of the bride Jacob thought he was getting. It was the custom of the country that the older sister should be married first.

As we look at Leah's life, I trust we will learn how we can do what is right, even when something that is wrong is done to us. Leah also shows us the example of a faithful wife in spite of bad circumstances at home.

Jacob Arrives at Laban's Home

Jacob had been running away from God, but on the way from his homeland to the land of his uncle Laban, he had a dream. Jacob named the place where he had the dream "Bethel," meaning house of God. God promised to keep Jacob wherever he went, and return him safely home. In turn, Jacob promised to serve the Lord and give back a tenth of all God gave him.

After Jacob left Bethel, he eventually reached his uncle Laban's house. On the way, he met his cousin Rachel tending sheep. It was love at first sight. When she realized Jacob was a relative, Rachel ran and told her father of the young man's arrival.

After Jacob told Laban all that had happened to him, his uncle warmly received him. Jacob wanted to work for his uncle, so they agreed that he would work for seven years in order to have Rachel for his wife.

Differences Between Rachel and Leah

Genesis 29:16–18 tells of the differences between the two sisters:

> [16] And Laban had two daughters: the name of the elder was Leah, and the name of the younger was Rachel.
> [17] Leah was tender eyed; but Rachel was beautiful and well favored.
> [18] And Jacob loved Rachel; and said, I will serve thee seven years for Rachel thy younger daughter.

The Bible does not describe Leah's eye problem. But it is obvious there was a striking physical difference between the two sisters. Jacob was attracted to Rachel.

Jacob Works in Order to Marry Rachel

Not only was Jacob attracted to Rachel, but the degree of his love for her is seen in Genesis 29:20: *"And Jacob served seven years for Rachel; and they seemed unto him but a few days, for the love he had to her."*

At the end of the seven years, Jacob reminded his uncle of the promise. The wedding was prepared. As was the custom, the bride was taken to the bedchamber of the groom in complete darkness and silence. Jacob did not realize until the next morning that he had been tricked by Laban, who had given him Leah instead of Rachel.

Laban's reason for his trickery was that he couldn't give the younger daughter in marriage before the older one. That was true according to local custom, but it is not what the two men had agreed upon earlier. Leah found herself married to the man who loved her sister. The Bible says that after Jacob spent a week with Leah, he got Rachel, too, but only after promising to work another seven years for his uncle Laban.

A Bad Situation

I cannot think of a worse situation. The Bible does not give the details of all the problems in the home, but it does discuss one in Genesis 29:30–31:

> [30] Jacob loved Rachel more than Leah, and served with him yet seven other years.
> [31] And when the LORD saw that Leah was hated, he opened her womb: but Rachel was barren.

God blessed Leah with children. Rachel had to listen to the crying and cooing of her sister's children while she had none.

Because Leah was not loved as much as Rachel, perhaps she spent more time drawing strength from God. The Bible states that Leah saw God's care for her in the birth of each child. Rachel had Jacob's love, but one thing is evident in Leah's life. In spite of her circumstances, she was a true and faithful wife. She did not turn her back on Jacob, nor did she give up trying to win his love.

Leah's attitude of praise to the Lord is revealed in the way she chose names for her sons as described in Genesis 29:32–35:

> [32] And Leah conceived, and bare a son, and she called his name Reuben: for she said, Surely the LORD hath looked upon my affliction; now therefore my husband will love me.
> [33] And she conceived again, and bare a son; and said, Because the LORD hath heard that I was hated, he

hath therefore given me this son also: and she called his name Simeon.

[34] And she conceived again, and bare a son; and said, Now this time will my husband be joined unto me, because I have born him three sons: therefore was his name called Levi.

[35] And she conceived again, and bare a son: and she said, Now will I praise the LORD: therefore she called his name Judah; and left bearing.

As we look further, through Genesis chapter 30, we see that Rachel became so jealous of Leah's children that she gave her maid Bilhah to Jacob to bear him children. Bilhah bore Jacob two more sons.

Then Leah gave her maid Zilpah to Jacob, and she also bore two sons. Later, Leah gave birth to two more sons and a daughter called Dinah, the first daughter in the Bible whose name is mentioned at birth.

At long last, Rachel gave birth to a son whom she named Joseph. As Rachel bore a second son, named Benjamin, she died. Hers is the first death due to childbirth recorded in the Bible.

Leah Blessed by the Lord

What happened to Leah? The Bible doesn't give many details, but we know she produced six sons who were the founders of one-half of the twelve tribes of Israel. Leah outlived her sister, and finally had her place as Jacob's only wife. The Lord continued to shower his blessings on Leah. From her son Judah came the Messianic line of King David, from which Jesus was born. From Leah also came the priestly tribe of Levi, from which Moses and Aaron descended.

CLOSING THOUGHTS

When I think of Leah, I think of a woman whose life represents an example of faithfulness to God, both while at her father's home and after she married. We never read of any complaints or bitterness either for her physical appearance or for the situation in her marriage. Apart from giving her maid to Jacob, Leah seems to have done what was right, and God blessed her.

This is a good time for us to examine our lives. Let us be challenged by Leah's life to be content in our circumstances, no matter what they are.

FOR DISCUSSION

1. In your own words, describe Leah's circumstances.
2. How does the Bible describe the differences between Leah and her sister?
3. Where do you think Leah and Rachel got the idea of having their maid servants give them children by their husband? What does that teach about being a good example to our children?
4. In what ways did God bless Leah?
5. Do you think Jacob ever loved Leah?

CHAPTER 9

DINAH

ATTRACTED BY THE WORLD

Most of the women in this Bible study are good examples for us to follow. There are a few, however, who made mistakes of judgment or were downright rebellious. They show us what we should not do.

Dinah is one of those. As the daughter of Jacob and Leah, she was part of a family under the covenant of God's blessing. The twelve tribes of Israel descended from her brothers.

Why Dinah Is a Bad Example

As Dinah and the rest of her family traveled from Paddan Aram to the city of Shechem in Canaan, Jacob bought a piece of land from Hamor, the prince of Shechem. Once they settled, Dinah decided to go see what life was like in Shechem. This attraction and curiosity caused a great deal of trouble and anguish. The true account is found in Genesis 34:1–2.

> [1] And Dinah the daughter of Leah, which she bare unto Jacob, went out to see the daughters of the land.
> [2] And when Shechem the son of Hamor the Hivite, prince of the country, saw her, he took her, and lay with her, and defiled her.

I am sure when Dinah left home to visit the "daughters" of the land, it was out of natural curiosity. The only girl in the family of eleven brothers, she did not use wisdom when she went, unprotected, into a strange city.

When Dinah appeared in Shechem alone, she was a prime target for the men of the city. The son of Hamor "saw her and took her," the Bible says. Some scholars believe the words "took her" in the Hebrew language of the Old Testament implies she was taken by force and raped.

Whatever the case, the prince of Shechem defiled her. The Bible doesn't say whether or not Dinah resisted or tried to get away from him. When a similar thing happened to her brother Joseph in Egypt, he fled, leaving his coat behind when Potiphar's wife tried to seduce him.

Genesis 34:3–8 tells the family's reaction when they found out what happened to Dinah:

> ³ And his soul clave unto Dinah the daughter of Jacob, and he loved the damsel, and spake kindly unto the damsel.
>
> ⁴ And Shechem spake unto his father Hamor, saying, Get me this damsel to wife.
>
> ⁵ And Jacob heard that he had defiled Dinah his daughter: now his sons were with his cattle in the field: and Jacob held his peace until they were come.
>
> ⁶ And Hamor the father of Shechem went out unto Jacob to commune with him.
>
> ⁷ And the sons of Jacob came out of the field when they heard it: and the men were grieved, and they were very wroth, because he had wrought folly in Israel in lying with Jacob's daughter; which thing ought not to be done.
>
> ⁸ And Hamor communed with them, saying, The soul of my son Shechem longeth for your daughter: I pray you give her him to wife.

It seems that Jacob, although grieved, wanted to work things out without causing a lot of trouble. But Dinah's brothers became very angry. They thought their sister had been treated like a harlot. In the middle of the account, the Bible adds the fact that the man who seduced Dinah was attracted enough to her that he wanted her for his wife.

Dinah's brothers made an agreement with the men of the country. They told them that Dinah could not marry an uncircumcised man. The men of the city got together and looked at the wealth of Jacob's family. They decided to be circumcised if that was all it took to get wives from that family. So "every man in the city was circumcised" (Genesis 34:24).

The men of Shechem changed their outward appearance, not to be pure before God or to identify themselves with the people of God, but rather to get wives from the Israelites. Men and women around the world are guilty of doing the same thing today. They will go to church, clean up their language, and stop bad habits, all to get a spouse, but never truly repent of their sins. We must warn our friends and our children of this danger so they will not be caught in the trap of marriage to an unbeliever.

Dinah's Brothers' Anger

The Bible goes on to say that even after all the men were circumcised, Dinah's brothers were still angry and not satisfied. The rest of the story is found in Genesis 34:24–27:

> [24] . . . and every male was circumcised, all that went out of the gate of his city.
>
> [25] And it came to pass on the third day, when they were sore, that two of the sons of Jacob, Simeon and Levi, Dinah's brethren, took each man his sword, and came upon the city boldly, and slew all the males.
>
> [26] And they slew Hamor and Shechem his son with the edge of the sword, and took Dinah out of Shechem's house, and went out.
>
> [27] The sons of Jacob came upon the slain, and spoiled the city, because they had defiled their sister.

Dinah's visit to the city not only cost her her virginity, but also the lives of many other people in Shechem. She was defiled as if she were a harlot, and in the end the man who defiled her died.

The story ends in a cruel and bloody mess. But one thing comes across clearly. The Israelites placed a high value on the chastity of their women.

In the next chapter of Genesis, we read that God told Jacob to take his family and go to Bethel to worship Him. Although her name is not specifically named, we can assume Dinah went along with her family. They all learned a valuable lesson from this tragedy.

Lessons for Us from Dinah's Life

What can we learn from this incident? First, we need to realize it is not wrong to be inquisitive about the world around us. God gave us minds to think, and He intends for us to use them. But it is wrong to put ourselves or others in danger just to satisfy our curiosity. Did Dinah ask her father's permission to make this visit? Did she ask one of her brothers to go with her? We don't know.

But we know that when we do anything contrary to God's Word it can lead to problems and possibly even disaster. 1 John 2:15–17 gives a solemn warning about loving the things of the world. Here is the command:

> [15] Love not the world, neither the things that are in the world. If any man love the world, the love of the Father is not in him.
>
> [16] For all that is in the world, the lust of the flesh, and the lust of the eyes, and the pride of life, is not of the Father, but is of the world.
>
> [17] And the world passeth away, and the lust thereof: but he that doeth the will of God abideth for ever.

Another lesson we can learn from Dinah is that God is full of love and mercy. After the tragedy, Dinah's family returned to

Bethel, where God had met with Jacob before. They worshiped God there together. 1 John 1:9 says: *"If we confess our sins, He is faithful and righteous to forgive us our sins and to cleanse us from all unrighteousness."*

We need to learn how to ask for and accept God's forgiveness; then we must move forward in our lives. We do not need to be continually defeated over a past failure.

CLOSING THOUGHTS

Often women make big mistakes in the matter of marriage. Even though they know the person they want to marry is not a true believer in Jesus Christ, they think somehow things will get better after they are married. They reason, "He'll go to church with me after we are married" or "He'll stop his heavy drinking and partying after we have settled into married life." Thinking along these lines, they take the risks of marrying an unbeliever instead of choosing to obey God's Word. What tragedy they bring into their lives.

Perhaps you have acted foolishly, like Dinah, and find yourself in a lot of trouble. If so, remember that God gives second chances. Do you think your situation is impossible to change? God is the God of the impossible. He can take a broken and battered life and breathe peace, freedom, and new hope into it. Turn to God today for the cleansing and help you need. Admit your sin and ask for forgiveness. Since God gave His only Son to die for your sin, will He not freely give you the help you need? You can be sure He will!

FOR DISCUSSION

1. What mistakes did Dinah make?
2. What was the result of her curiosity?
3. How did Dinah's brothers react to what happened to their sister?

4. What was the significance of the family's returning to Bethel?

5. What hope is there for those who have gotten into troubles of their own making?

CHAPTER 10

MIRIAM

JEALOUSY BRINGS JUDGMENT

What qualities come to mind when you think of a leader? Can Christian women hold a place of leadership? Among the answers to the questions of what makes a leader, we might say: a person who takes charge during a crisis, one who motivates others to do their best, a quick thinker, a decision-maker, or someone with vision.

Do women make good leaders? In the Bible, God gives several examples of women who were in positions of leadership. Miriam is one of them.

Miriam's Childhood

Miriam had an older brother named Aaron, and a younger brother named Moses. Moses was the man God chose to lead the nation of Israel out of slavery in Egypt into the land He had promised them. Miriam was a dynamic leader and a prophetess. Unfortunately, she became jealous of Moses and ended her life showing the entire nation of Israel how jealousy brings sorrow.

The Bible tells one account from Miriam's childhood. Her mother sent her to watch over her baby brother, Moses. He was placed in a boat-like basket in the river to protect him from Pharaoh, the king, who had ordered that all Hebrew baby boys were to be killed. Even as a child, Miriam displayed leadership characteristics in a difficult situation. Exodus 2:4–10 explains:

⁴ And his sister stood afar off, to wit what would be done to him.

⁵ And the daughter of Pharaoh came down to wash
herself at the river, and her maidens walked along by
the river's side; and when she saw the ark among the
flags, she sent her maid to fetch it.

⁶ And when she had opened it, she saw the child:
and, behold, the baby wept. And she had compassion
on him, and said, This is one of the Hebrews' children.

⁷ Then said his sister to Pharaoh's daughter, Shall I go
and call to thee a nurse of the Hebrew women, that
she may nurse the child for thee?

⁸ And Pharaoh's daughter said to her, Go. And the
maid went and called the child's mother.

⁹ And Pharaoh's daughter said to her, Take this child
away and nurse it for me, and I will give thee thy
wages. And the woman took the child, and nursed it.

¹⁰ And the child grew, and she brought him unto
Pharaoh's daughter, and he became her son. And she
called his name Moses: and she said, Because I drew
him out of the water.

Miriam had come from a God-fearing home. Imagine how
Miriam's mother explained to her that God would take care of
her baby brother. Miriam had a sense of responsibility at a young
age. She knew her family was in danger because they hid her
brother from Pharaoh. Yet in difficult circumstances, when the
right time came, she was calm, quick thinking, and spoke wisely.
She didn't even identify her mother to the princess.

Nothing more is said about Miriam until many years later
when her brother, Moses, led the children of Israel out of Egypt.
We know, however, that Miriam lived in Egypt as a slave, and that
she must have had a hard life as did the other Israelites under
Pharaoh's rule.

Miriam: A Prophetess

The next time Miriam is mentioned is in Exodus 15:20. She is called the sister of Aaron and a prophetess, a position of responsibility given by God.

After Moses led the children of Israel out of Egypt, his brother, Aaron, became the high priest, representing the people before God. It appears that Miriam was also in a place of leadership. Her responsibilities included music. Today, she might be called the worship team leader. After the Israelites crossed the Red Sea on dry ground and the Egyptian army drowned, Miriam led the women in the praise song recorded in Exodus 15:20–21:

> ²⁰ And Miriam the prophetess, the sister of Aaron,
> took a timbrel in her hand; and all the women went
> out after her with timbrels and with dances.
> ²¹ And Miriam answered them, Sing ye to the Lord,
> for he hath triumphed gloriously: the horse and his
> rider hath he thrown into the sea.

Miriam's gift was singing, and she used her gift. Perhaps she lifted the spirits of the people many times as they walked through the wilderness by leading them in songs of praise. It is good for us to get into the habit of using our gifts to remind each other of God's faithfulness to all of us. In Hebrews 10:24-25 we read:

> ²⁴ And let us consider one another to provoke unto
> love and good works:
> ²⁵ Not forsaking the assembling of ourselves together,
> as the manner of some is; but exhorting one another
> and so much the more, as ye see the day approaching.

Miriam's Jealousy

While Moses lived in a foreign country, he married a woman from that country. She was not an Israelite. Because of this marriage, Miriam and her brother Aaron rebelled against Moses.

They challenged the leadership position God had given him. In Numbers 12:2 the brother and sister asked, *"Has the Lord indeed spoken only through Moses? Has he not spoken through us as well?"*

We find no record that Moses became angry and answered his older brother and sister harshly. In fact, Scripture describes Moses this way, *"Moses was very humble, more than any man who was on the face of the earth"* (Numbers 12:3).

Miriam's Judgment

Of course, the Lord heard what was said. In response to this challenge to Moses' authority, the Lord called Aaron, Miriam, and Moses together. God came down in a cloud to meet with them. Because of Miriam's jealousy and unwillingness to follow the leader God had chosen, He caused her to be stricken with the most feared disease of that day—leprosy. Moses pleaded for his sister's healing, even though she had spoken against him. The Lord answered, but not without making sure Miriam realized how wicked her rebellion had been. Numbers 12:15 tells us: *"Miriam was shut up outside the camp for seven days, and the people did not move on until Miriam was received again."*

From this account, we see how God heard and saw the complaints of Miriam and Aaron. He answered them in person. He made it very clear that they had been wrong; they had sinned. Moses was God's chosen leader.

How humiliating it must have been for Miriam to be the camp outcast for seven days. She had time to think, and to seek God's forgiveness for her jealousy and rebellion.

After the seven days, and her recovery from leprosy, there is no further mention of Miriam or the service she may have given to the Israelites. It is believed Miriam died shortly after this incident, before the Israelites entered the Promised Land.

CLOSING THOUGHTS

The greatest example God gave us of a leader was His Son, the Lord Jesus Christ. Although He was a leader, He also showed the perfect example of how to serve. Jesus said: *"Whosoever will be chief among you, let him be your servant"* (Matthew 20:27).

What does this mean for us? God has given each of us a job to do for Him. Are we doing it with joy, as we should do? Or are we jealous of the job someone else has been given? Do we want more than God has given us? It is important to learn to be content with our gifts and to use them for God, without comparing ourselves with other people and their gifts or service for the Lord.

FOR DISCUSSION

1. What leadership qualities were evident in Miriam's life even as a child?
2. Describe Miriam's attitude according to Numbers 12:2.
3. What leadership qualities did Moses show when he was criticized?
4. In Matthew 20:25–28, how did Jesus describe a true leader?
5. Name two good examples we can follow from the lives of both Miriam and Moses.

CHAPTER 11

PHARAOH'S DAUGHTER

SIMPLY USED OF GOD

Most of the time we think of God using great women of faith such as Mary, Sarah, Esther. But the Bible clearly teaches that God uses whomever and whatever He chooses to accomplish His perfect plan. Pharaoh's daughter is a good example of this truth.

Background on Pharaoh's Daughter

She was an Egyptian woman who did not worship the true God. As did the rest of her people, she probably worshiped Ra, the sun god, and many other idols. Her father, the ruler of Egypt, did not have any respect or love for the Hebrew God of Abraham, Isaac, and Jacob.

She is not named in the Bible. She is simply referred to as "Pharaoh's daughter," possibly because she was his only daughter.

The Sad Situation of the Hebrews in Egypt

God's chosen people, the Israelites, were slaves in Egypt. They had a hard life under cruel masters, yet their numbers grew so rapidly that Pharaoh felt threatened. He was afraid if they became too big a nation they might try to overthrow his government, or would join with an invading army to fight against him. To prevent this, he made a law to kill all the baby boys born to their women.

This was a terrible law, and brought great sorrow. One family, however, showed faith and trust in God when their baby boy was born. They refused to kill him. The Bible says they hid the child for three months.

How God Used Pharaoh's Daughter

Exodus 2:3–6 tells how almighty God used Pharaoh's daughter for His eternal purpose:

> ³ And when she could not longer hide him, she took for him an ark of bulrushes, and daubed it with slime and with pitch, and put the child therein; and she laid it in the flags by the river's brink.
>
> ⁴ And his sister stood afar off, to wit what would be done to him.
>
> ⁵ And the daughter of Pharaoh came down to wash herself at the river; and her maidens walked along by the river's side; and when she saw the ark among the flags, she sent her maid to fetch it.
>
> ⁶ And when she had opened it, she saw the child: and, behold, the babe wept. And she had compassion on him, and said, This is one of the Hebrews' children.

One lesson we who are believers in Christ so quickly forget and yet desperately need to remember is that God is sovereign. We should live with this thought in mind: God is in control at all times. He has a plan and a purpose for each of us. Psalm 135:5–6 says: *"For I know that the LORD is great, and that our Lord is above all gods. Whatsoever the LORD pleased, that did he in heaven, and in earth, in the seas, and all deep places."*

When Pharaoh's daughter saw the tears of baby Moses, she felt compassion. In doing this, she was being used by God, although she did not know it. Her qualities of kindness, love, and concern for the child are in sharp contrast to her father's cruelty.

This Egyptian princess risked her own life for a child whom the Pharaoh had ordered to be killed. She showed strong character when she defied her father's order. Romans chapter 1 explains that God's laws are made plain to all mankind, so she knew it was cruel and unjust to murder the baby she found in the bulrushes.

God's Sovereign Providence

When the princess decided to save the baby's life, she accepted his sister's offer to get someone to care for him. The princess liked that idea, and Moses' own mother was paid to raise her son for Pharaoh's daughter. Once again, we see that God was in complete control.

The Bible then says in Exodus 2:10, *"And the child grew, and she brought him unto Pharaoh's daughter, and he became her son. And she called his name Moses: and she said, Because I drew him out of the water."*

The New Testament confirms how Pharaoh's daughter was used by God to provide education and training for Moses. That preparation proved invaluable when he led God's children out of Egypt. The verses in Acts 7:21–22 say: *"Pharaoh's daughter took him up, and nourished him for her own son. And Moses was learned in all the wisdom of the Egyptians, and was mighty in words and in deeds."*

Moses Adopted by Pharaoh's Daughter

What these verses really say is that Pharaoh's daughter adopted Moses. She took him and cared for him as her own son. She named him and gave him all she could in the way of knowledge, education, and wealth. Without doubt, she gave him much love as he grew up under her care.

It must have been a sad day for the princess when Moses refused to be known as her son. He returned to the Israelites and was the human instrument who redeemed them from slavery.

The Bible does not tell us whether the princess ever saw her adopted son again. But we can praise the Lord today for her part in preparing Moses for God's service.

God Prepared a Savior for You

Just as God in His sovereign control arranged for Moses to redeem the Israelites from Egyptian slavery, He provided Jesus

Christ as a Savior for you. Jesus died on the Cross for your sin, and if you trust Him, He will forgive you and free you from spiritual slavery. If you want joy and peace and freedom from spiritual bondage, admit you are a sinner, and believe in and receive the Lord Jesus Christ as your Savior.

CLOSING THOUGHTS

You may already have trusted in Jesus but are living in difficult circumstances just as Moses' parents did. Or perhaps, as in the account we have just studied, God has sent into your life a person who has been a help to you but is not a believer in the true God. Ask God to help you be a witness to that person. It is a comfort to know our heavenly Father is in control of everything. 1 Chronicles 29:10–12 makes this clear: *"Blessed be thou, LORD God of Israel our father, for ever and ever. Thine, O LORD, is the greatness, and the power, and the glory, and the victory, and the majesty: for all that is in the heaven and in the earth is thine; thine is the kingdom, O LORD, and thou art exalted as head above all. Both riches and honour come of thee, and thou reignest over all; and in thine hand is power and might; and in thine hand it is to make great, and to give strength unto all."*

FOR DISCUSSION

1. What personality characteristics did Pharaoh's daughter have?
2. How did her life show the difference between the law of God and the law of man?
3. What qualities did Moses' family display?
4. Name three ways God used Pharaoh's daughter in Moses' life.
5. Describe a specific time in your life when you saw or personally experienced God's sovereignty.

CHAPTER 12

RAHAB

A CHANGED HARLOT

Many women have lived through events and experiences in the past that cause problems in their lives now. It may be a difficult childhood, a husband who deserted her, failure at a job, or the death of someone close. If those who have lived through such difficult experiences allow bitterness or anger to grow in their hearts, their spiritual growth and development may be slowed down or come to a complete halt.

God's Word tells the story of Rahab as an illustration of a completely changed life. After she trusted in the God of Israel, everything from her past was forgiven—even physically destroyed. By faith, Rahab moved on into a victorious life.

Rahab Makes Her Choice

The story of Rahab is recorded in Joshua chapter two. Before conquering the land God had promised for His chosen people, Joshua sent two spies to explore the city of Jericho. They found lodging in a house on the city wall where the harlot, Rahab, lived. The Bible does not tell us why the spies went to her house, but it does tell us that she protected them by hiding them on the roof.

Between the time the spies came to Rahab's house and the time the king of Jericho heard they were in the city, Rahab must have made her confession of faith in the true God to the spies. Rahab knew what had happened to God's people after they left

Egypt. She believed in Israel's God, and proved her faith by risking her life to help the spies who were enemies of Jericho.

Rahab's Faith Shown in Her Works

Even though they were in enemy territory, the spies shared their faith with Rahab. God honored their boldness and He used Rahab to help them in two ways:

- She saved the lives of the spies, and
- she encouraged their faith by telling them of the reputation of God's people.

Joshua 2:9 and 2:24 tell how this news spread and encouraged even Joshua himself.

> [9] And she said unto the men, I know that the Lord hath given you the land, and that your terror is fallen upon us, and that all the inhabitants of the land faint because of you.
> [24] And they said unto Joshua, Truly the Lord hath delivered into our hands all the land; for even all the inhabitants of the country do faint because of us.

Rahab was saved by faith in the true God, but she showed this faith through her work of saving the lives of the spies. The New Testament speaks of Rahab's faith in James 2:25–26: *"Likewise also was not Rahab the harlot justified by works, when she had received the messengers, and had sent them out another way? For as the body without the spirit is dead, so faith without works is dead also."*

Hebrews 11, known as the great faith chapter of the Bible, speaks of Rahab's faith in verse 31: *"By faith the harlot Rahab perished not with them that believed not, when she had received the spies with peace."*

Rahab's Immediate Reward

In exchange for helping the spies, Rahab asked that they not kill her and her family. The spies agreed. After she let them out over the city wall by a rope through the window, the spies told

her to tie a scarlet cord in her window. They promised that whoever was in her house would be kept alive. Joshua 6:21–25 gives
the account of what happened when the battle of Jericho actually took place:

> ²¹ And they utterly destroyed all that was in the city,
> both man and woman, young and old, and ox, and
> sheep, and ass, with the edge of the sword.
>
> ²² But Joshua had said unto the two men that had
> spied out the country, Go into the harlot's house, and
> bring out thence the woman, and all that she hath as
> ye sware unto her.
>
> ²³ And the young men that were spies went in, and
> brought out Rahab, and her father, and her mother,
> and her brethren, and all that she had; and they brought
> out all her kindred, and left them without the camp of
> Israel.
>
> ²⁴ And they burnt the city with fire, and all that was
> therein: only the silver and the gold, and the vessels
> of brass and of iron, they put into the treasury of the
> house of the Lord.
>
> ²⁵ And Joshua saved Rahab the harlot alive, and
> her father's household, and all that she had; and she
> dwelleth in Israel even unto this day; because she hid
> the messengers which Joshua sent to spy out Jericho.

CLOSING THOUGHTS

Rahab's faith and completely changed life should make us
think about our own lives. Her faith must have been so real that
her whole family believed her story. They were in the house
with her when the walls of Jericho fell. Rahab lost all her friends
and lived as a stranger in the camp of Israel, but God honored her
faith. Physically, her life was spared. Spiritually, her works proved
her faith and God declared her justified (James 2:25). Even

beyond that, Rahab's name is included in the list of the ancestors of Jesus Christ (Matthew 1:5).

Rahab's life is a reminder of God's continuing grace. God doesn't wait until we are perfect before He uses us. He takes us just as we are, regardless of our past. As we declare our faith, God works out His plan.

FOR DISCUSSION

1. List three specific ways God used Rahab.
2. What qualities in Rahab's life would you like to have in your own life?
3. How were Rahab's life and circumstances changed?
4. In what way has God changed your life since you accepted Jesus Christ as your Savior?
5. How does your life show others the power of God's forgiveness?

CHAPTER 13

ACHSAH

A WISE BRIDE

Achsah may not be a familiar name to many people, but she had some of the important qualities of the Proverbs 31 woman who was praised for her keen business abilities and her devotion to her family. Achsah was the daughter of Caleb. Her husband, Othniel, became one of Israel's judges (Judges 3:8–11).

Background

Just before the Israelites went into the land God had promised to give them, their leader, Moses, sent twelve spies to check out the land. Caleb was one of those spies. When the spies returned, they said the land was flowing with milk and honey, and they even brought some fruit to prove it. But ten of the spies said the people of the land were too powerful to fight. Caleb and his friend, Joshua, however, were brave because they had faith in God's promise. They encouraged the Israelites to conquer the land as God had told them to.

Those who did not believe God died in the wilderness between Egypt and the Promised Land. Because of their faith in God, Caleb and Joshua lived and went into the Promised Land (Numbers 26:65). Later, as the land was divided among the people, Caleb became the prince of the tribe of Judah (Numbers 34:18–19). He was given the town of Hebron for his inheritance (Joshua 14:13).

Caleb is the father of the woman we are considering in this study. Caleb was a man who had great faith in God. No doubt

Achsah often heard of the many things God had done for her people when they left the land of Egypt, and how He provided for them in the wilderness.

The Importance of Achsah's Story

Achsah's story is short, yet important enough for God to have included the account in two books of the Old Testament: Joshua and Judges. The account of Achsah begins when she was old enough to marry. Both Joshua 15:16-19 and Judges 1:12-15 state:

> [16] And Caleb said, He that smiteth Kirjathsepher, and taketh it, to him will I give Achsah my daughter to wife.
> [17] And Othniel the son of Kenaz, the brother of Caleb, took it: and he gave him Achsah his daughter to wife.
> [18] And it came to pass, as she came unto him, that she moved him to ask of her father a field: and she lighted off her ass; and Caleb said unto her, What wouldest thou?
> [19] Who answered, Give me a blessing; for thou hast given me a south land; give me also springs of water. And he gave her the upper springs, and the nether springs.

Because Caleb was a man of God, I do not think he deliberately gave his daughter poor land. Perhaps he did not personally examine the land, but had taken the word of a steward as to the condition of the land. In any case, the "south land" (possibly the area today known as the Negev) was arid and parched. Land without sufficient water supply was next to useless. Achsah asked only for water, without which the ground she had would be of little use.

A Wise and Prudent Woman

In this short account, we find a bride who was not content to settle for a struggling existence. As a woman interested in the welfare of her family, she persuaded her husband they should have more than the dry desert land given to them by her father. While Achsah had good insight into the situation, she did not simply take matters into her own hands. She respected her husband and asked him to speak to her father about the matter. We don't know why he was reluctant to ask. Achsah, as the beloved daughter about to leave home, was in the position to ask.

Because Caleb recognized the fairness of his daughter's request, he granted her wish. He gave her what she asked for, and more. She asked for springs of water, which naturally included the field where the springs were located. Her father not only gave her the upper springs, but the lower springs also.

Spiritual Blessings

The upper and lower springs Caleb gave his daughter have been used as word pictures of God's rich blessing toward us. Our heavenly Father promises to give us the desires of our hearts. Then He goes beyond and gives us more than we can imagine. *"Now unto him that is able to do exceeding abundantly above all that we ask or think, according to the power that worketh in us"* (Ephesians 3:20).

God's supply never runs out, and He delights in making His children happy. As His children, we need to learn that we can come boldly to Him in prayer and lay before Him both our needs and our desires. Here are some verses to remind us of God's generous supply of our needs, whether they are spiritual or material:

- *"Blessed be the God and Father of our Lord Jesus Christ, who hath blessed us with all spiritual blessings in heavenly places in Christ Jesus"* (Ephesians 1:3).

- *"For the LORD God is a sun and shield: the LORD will give grace and glory: no good thing will he withhold from them that walk uprightly"* (Psalm 84:11).
- *"Every good gift and every perfect gift is from above, and cometh down from the Father of lights, with whom is no variableness, neither shadow of turning"* (James 1:17).

CLOSING THOUGHTS

Perhaps you are worried about a need in your family. I believe the story of Achsah is included in the Bible as a reminder of how strong a father's love is. Caleb gave his daughter what she asked for—and more. In the same way, our heavenly Father cares for us. He does not like to see us suffer and He wants to give us good gifts.

But the Scriptures also state requirements for receiving God's good gifts.

- Psalm 66:18 warns us, *"If I regard iniquity in my heart, the Lord will not hear."*
- James 4:2–3 explains that we do not have what we want because we do not ask God. Or, when we do ask, we do not receive because we ask with the wrong motives— wanting to spend the gift for our own pleasure rather than for God's glory.
- In each of the Gospels, we read the account of the Lord Jesus when He prayed in the garden of Gethsemane. As Jesus prayed to His Father, He said, *"Not My will, but Thine be done."*

When we confess our sins and pray with clean hearts and proper motives, always asking for God's will to be done, He will hear and answer in the way that is best for us.

Make a list of all the things God has either done for you or given to you in the last week, month, and year. Don't forget to include answered prayers. If you are married, review the list with your husband. Then pray together and thank the Lord for all He has done. It may surprise you how much God has already done for you!

FOR DISCUSSION

1. Describe Achsah's home life both before and after her marriage.
2. What qualities listed in Proverbs 31 do you see in Achsah's life?
3. In what ways did she show her practical wisdom?
4. In what two ways are Caleb and our heavenly Father similar?
5. Give two reasons why you think Achsah's story is included in the Bible.

CHAPTER 14

DEBORAH

A LEADER BLESSED OF GOD

Deborah was a woman who became a judge in Israel. She was known throughout Israel for her godly counsel and wisdom. But Deborah became much more than just a counselor; she led the Israelites to victory in battle against their enemies.

The Time of the Judges

Deborah lived in the difficult time in Israel's history after Joshua's death and before the nation had an earthly king. God chose Joshua, after Moses's death, to lead the Israelites into the Promised Land. There, however, they developed a sad pattern of behavior: rebellion against God, defeat at the hands of their enemies, and crying out to God in repentance. In response to their cries, God would raise up a judge to deliver them and give them victory over their enemies. After a period of peace and prosperity, the cycle repeated itself: rebellion, defeat, repentance, deliverance, and peace.

It is important to understand what the Bible says about judges, so we can more fully appreciate the lessons to be learned from Deborah. Judges 2:16 and 2:18 explain:

> [16] Nevertheless the LORD raised up judges, which delivered them out of the hand of those that spoiled them.
> [17] And when the LORD raised them up judges, then the LORD was with the judge, and delivered them out

of the hand of their enemies all the days of the judge: for it repented the LORD because of their groanings by reason of them that oppressed them and vexed them.

Deborah was the fifth judge of the Israelites. The people knew she was appointed and blessed by God. She had great faith in God and believed He would rescue His people if they honored Him.

Deborah, a Judge

The story of Deborah is found in Judges chapters 4 and 5. Once again, the people of Israel had rebelled against the Lord. Because of this, they suffered 20 years of oppression from enemy rule.

God's Word gives very little information about Deborah. Judges 4:4 states the only personal information we know. It says she was married to Lappidoth, that she was a prophetess, and *"she judged Israel at that time."*

As you read Judges 4:5–9, 13, 16 keep in mind that Deborah was a judge, a wife, and a prophetess who made God's will known to man.

⁵ And she dwelt under the palm tree of Deborah between Ramah and Bethel in mount Ephraim: and the children of Israel came up to her for judgment.

⁶ And she sent and called Barak the son of Abinoam out of Kedeshnaphtali, and said unto him, Hath not the LORD God of Israel commanded, saying, Go and draw toward mount Tabor, and take with thee ten thousand men of the children of Naphtali and of the children of Zebulun?

⁷ And I will draw unto thee to the river Kishon Sisera, the captain of Jabin's army, with his chariots and his multitude; and I will deliver him into thine hand.

⁸ And Barak said unto her, If thou wilt go with me,

then I will go: but if thou wilt not go with me, then
I will not go.

⁹ And she said, I will surely go with thee: notwithstanding the journey that thou takest shall not be for
thine honour; for the LORD shall sell Sisera into the
hand of a woman. And Deborah arose, and went with
Barak to Kedesh.

¹³ And Sisera gathered together all his chariots, even
nine hundred chariots of iron, and all the people that
were with him . . .

¹⁶ But Barak pursued after the chariots, and after the
host, unto Harosheth of the Gentiles: and all the host
of Sisera fell upon the edge of the sword; and there was
not a man left.

The story concludes with the killing of Sisera at the hands of
a woman named Jael. God brought about a great victory for His
people. All that Deborah prophesied came true. Because of this,
we know she was one of God's true prophets. One proof that a
prophet came from God was that all his (or her) words proved to
be true.

Qualifications of a Prophet of God

Many people today claim to be prophets from God. God's
Word gives guidelines so we can know who is a real prophet and
who is not. In Deuteronomy, God gave many of the laws His
people were to follow when they entered the Promised Land.
Deuteronomy 18:21–22 says this about prophets:

²¹ And if thou say in thine heart, How shall we know
the word which the LORD hath not spoken?

²² When a prophet speaketh in the name of the
LORD, if the thing follow not, nor come to pass, that
is the thing which the LORD hath not spoken, but the
prophet hath spoken it presumptuously: thou shalt not
be afraid of him.

Deuteronomy 13:1–3 gives another guideline that even if a prophet's predictions *do* come true but he tries to lead people away from the God of the Scriptures, he is not a true prophet:

> ¹ If there arise among you a prophet, or a dreamer of dreams, and giveth thee a sign or a wonder,
>
> ² And the sign or the wonder come to pass, whereof he spake unto thee, saying, Let us go after other gods, which thou hast not known, and let us serve them;
>
> ³ Thou shalt not hearken unto the words of that prophet, or that dreamer of dreams: for the LORD your God proveth you, to know whether ye love the LORD your God with all your heart and with all your soul.

Anyone who says he is a prophet from God must prove it by the fact that his prophecies always come true. Even then, the rest of his teaching must be examined. If his prophecies do not come true, or if he attempts to lead people away from God, God warns that this person is not a true prophet.

Deborah's Response to the Victory

Deborah responded to the victory God gave by singing a beautiful duet with Barak. In Judges 5, we find they gave all the praise to the Lord because He saved Israel. Even after the victory, Deborah remained true to God. She did not become proud, but continued to guide the children of Israel according to His laws. Judges 5:31b says, *"And the land had rest forty years."*

Deborah accepted her God-given role and her gift of leadership. She was God's chosen judge, and after the tremendous victory she continued her responsibilities.

Sometimes, when God allows us to use our gifts to do a task for Him, we get proud about our abilities. Or we think, *I've done my part, now let someone else do the work.* Neither of these is the correct attitude; we must continue using the gifts God has given us.

CLOSING THOUGHTS

Deborah knew it was God who would give victory, so she trusted Him to do it. In doing so, she could declare the victory with confidence. In the same way, we must read God's promises in His Word and then claim victory over the enemy in our lives.

Deborah's battle was against actual human enemies. Today, believers in Christ fight a spiritual battle against pride, lustful thoughts, and other sins. Is there some area in your spiritual life where you need to claim victory as Deborah and Barak did against Israel's enemies? God's Word tells how we can have victory over sin. We must claim God's promises. How do we do that?

- KNOW God's promises. We must regularly read or listen to God's Word. If we do not know God's promises, how can we claim them?
- BELIEVE that God will do as He promised.
- THANK God for His promises as we talk to Him in prayer.

1 Corinthians 15:57 says, *"But thanks be to God, which giveth us the victory through our Lord Jesus Christ."* God promises victory, so we can depend on Him and thank Him in advance.

God is the solution to the problems in our lives. Believe the words in Psalm 18:2–3 which talk about the sureness and the dependableness of God our deliverer: *"The LORD is my rock, and my fortress, and my deliverer; my God, my strength, in whom I will trust; my buckler, and the horn of my salvation, and my high tower. I will call upon the LORD, who is worthy to be praised: so shall I be saved from mine enemies."*

FOR DISCUSSION

1. Name three qualities seen in the life of Deborah.
2. How many of Deborah's predictions came true?
   Why is this significant?
3. Describe the battle plan.

4. Who received credit for the victory?
5. In your life, how can you claim victory in your spiritual battles?

CHAPTER 15

DELILAH

SHE BETRAYED FOR MONEY

Delilah is seen only briefly in Scripture. The Bible gives no record of her parents, and very little about her background. We know she came from the valley of Sorek, which lays west of Jerusalem in the country of the Philistines.

It is impossible to study the life of Delilah without including her involvement with Samson, a man of God who fell in love with her. Delilah accepted money from the Philistines to betray him. Samson and Delilah are distinctly different in character.

Samson

Samson was born to godly Israelite parents. From his birth, God blessed Samson with unusual strength because both he and his parents kept their vow to God. This vow, written in Numbers 6:2–12, included never cutting his hair. Samson became a judge in Israel during the time the Philistines were their enemies. Samson judged Israel for 20 years.

Samson was a man whom God had blessed with great physical strength, but he was morally weak. He won military battles and wrestled with a lion and won. But he could not control his own lusts or resist the charms of a woman.

Delilah: Her Character

Delilah was a deceitful woman who capitalized on her beauty. In her relationship with Samson, she used her charm, mental abilities, commanding attitude, and boldness for one purpose only—money.

Delilah was offered 1,100 pieces of silver by each of the Philistine lords as a bribe to find the secret of Samson's strength. This was a huge temptation. You may remember that Judas Iscariot was given only 30 pieces of silver to betray God's only Son, Jesus Christ. What a contrast: God's Son, of infinite value, betrayed for so little, while Samson was betrayed for so much more.

We know God would not have included this story in His Word if there were no lessons or principles for us to learn. Judges 16:4–5 says about Samson:

> ⁴ And it came to pass afterward, that he loved a woman in the valley of Sorek, whose name was Delilah.
>
> ⁵ And the lords of the Philistines came up unto her, and said unto her, Entice him, and see wherein his great strength lieth, and by what means we may prevail against him, that we may bind him to afflict him: and we will give thee every one of us eleven hundred pieces of silver.

Remember, Samson was Israel's leader at this time, and the Philistines were Israel's enemy. In previous lessons we learned God commanded the Israelite men not to marry women from the countries around them. Samson, however, had a weakness for Philistine women. The Philistines knew the only way they could ever destroy Samson would be through this weakness. So they agreed to pay Delilah to learn the secret of Samson's strength. She was willing to use her charms to betray his love for her.

Delilah: Her Persistence

The Bible tells us that before Delilah learned the truth about Samson's strength, she failed three times because Samson lied to her. Yet she persisted to beg him for his secret. Judges 16:15–20 states what happened the fourth time Delilah asked:

¹⁵ And she said unto him, How canst thou say, I love thee, when thine heart is not with me? thou hast mocked me these three times, and hast not told me wherein thy great strength lieth.

¹⁶ And it came to pass, when she pressed him daily with her words, and urged him, so that his soul was vexed unto death;

¹⁷ That he told her all his heart, and said unto her, There hath not come a razor upon mine head; for I have been a Nazarite unto God from my mother's womb: if I be shaven, then my strength will go from me, and I shall become weak, and be like any other man.

¹⁸ And when Delilah saw that he had told her all his heart, she sent and called for the lords of the Philistines, saying, Come up this once, for he hath shewed me all his heart. Then the lords of the Philistines came up unto her, and brought money in their hand.

¹⁹ And she made him sleep upon her knees; and she called for a man, and she caused him to shave off the seven locks of his head; and she began to afflict him, and his strength went from him.

²⁰ And she said, The Philistines be upon thee, Samson. And he awoke out of his sleep, and said, I will go out as at other times before, and shake myself. And he wist not that the LORD was departed from him.

Delilah is never again mentioned in the Bible. We can only assume that once she got her money, she disappeared with it.

A Warning

What can we learn from this tragic story? Delilah stands out as an eternal warning to men to beware the dangers of a wicked and scheming but charming woman. In the book of Proverbs,

King Solomon gives many warnings about the ways of such a woman. For example, read Proverbs 7:4–5, 21–23, 25–27:

> [4] Say unto wisdom, Thou art my sister; and call understanding thy kinswoman:
>
> [5] That they may keep thee from the strange woman, from the stranger which flattereth with her words.
>
> [21] With her much fair speech she caused him to yield, with the flattering of her lips she forced him.
>
> [22] He goeth after her straightway, as an ox goeth to the slaughter, or as a fool to the correction of the stocks;
>
> [23] Till a dart strike through his liver; as a bird hasteth to the snare, and knoweth not that it is for his life.
>
> [25] Let not thine heart decline to her ways, go not astray in her paths.
>
> [26] For she hath cast down many wounded: yea, many strong men have been slain by her.
>
> [27] Her house is the way to hell, going down to the chambers of death.

These are powerful words from God. Women are in a unique position to guide children, whether as mothers, aunts, grandmothers, or teachers. Young men need to know how to avoid the trap into which Samson fell. Young women also need to be instructed how to use their beauty and charm as God intended, rather than for enticing men.

Remember, God will not be mocked. Samson failed to keep the important principle of not marrying someone from the surrounding pagan nations. The same principle is repeated in the New Testament in 2 Corinthians 6:14: *"Be ye not unequally yoked together with unbelievers: for what fellowship hath righteousness with unrighteousness? And what communion hath light with darkness?"*

Samson, a believer, bound himself to an unbeliever. If Samson had married an Israelite woman as his parents wanted, the tragedy of Delilah would never have happened. Instead, he married into a wicked nation and paid for this sin with his life.

CLOSING THOUGHTS

Delilah's story reminds us that even God's chosen people are capable of being deceived. We need to constantly renew our commitment to God. Perhaps one of the saddest parts of this story was that Samson did not even know God had left him. Consider your own situation. Have you given yourself in total surrender to Jesus Christ? Are you aware of His presence in your life? If not, receive Him as Savior, then give your life back to God so He can use you for His glory.

FOR DISCUSSION

1. Name two each of Samson's character strengths and weaknesses.
2. Name two each of Delilah's character strengths and weaknesses.
3. What does the Bible say about a deceitful woman?
4. What principle from God's Word did Samson violate?
5. What can you do in your own family to prevent a marriage with an unbeliever?

CHAPTER 16

NAOMI

A WISE MOTHER-IN-LAW

Naomi was a Jewish woman who lived more than 1,000 years before Christ's birth. Her story, along with that of her Gentile daughter-in-law, Ruth, is told in the book of Ruth. This Old Testament book gives much information about the culture and life of the people of that time.

Naomi: Her Life and Family

Naomi lived with her husband in the small town of Bethlehem in Judah, a province in the nation of Israel. At that time, Israel was ruled by a series of judges who were chosen by God to lead the Israelites. A great famine occurred in Judah, so Naomi's husband took her and their two sons to the land of Moab, a neighboring country whose people did not worship the true God.

Things were not easy for Naomi in Moab. She had been taken out of her homeland to live in a foreign country. She was a woman who sincerely loved God and His people, and revered His laws. But now she was far away from all that. If you have ever moved and had to settle in a new place, you can easily identify with what Naomi must have experienced. As if these weren't enough problems, Naomi's husband and sons died. We read about this in Ruth 1:3–5:

> ³ And Elimelech Naomi's husband died; and she was
> left, and her two sons.

⁴ And they took them wives of the women of Moab; the name of the one was Orpah, and the name of the other Ruth: and they dwelled there about ten years.

⁵ And Mahlon and Chilion died also both of them; and the woman was left of her two sons and her husband.

Naomi's life was filled with grief. She not only had to provide for herself, she now had two widowed daughters-in-law. They may have given their mother-in-law some comfort, but Orpah and Ruth were Moabites who did not share Naomi's faith in God.

Naomi Returns to Bethlehem

After the death of her sons, Naomi heard that the famine in Judah was over. She had no reason to stay in Moab, so she decided to return to Bethlehem. Her two daughters-in-law went with her. On the way, Naomi stopped and pleaded with them to return to their own homes.

Obviously, these women were more attached to their mother-in-law than to their own people. I think this shows Naomi was a godly woman and a kind mother-in-law. The daughters-in-law were willing to leave their own country to go with Naomi to her homeland. Her testimony about God must have been very clear.

According to the law, a man could marry his brother's widow if she was childless. In that way, the widow would produce an heir for the family. Naomi knew she was too old to have more sons to give as husbands to her daughters-in-law. She had no way of providing husbands or families for them. If they stayed in Moab, perhaps they could marry and have children. So, even though Naomi loved the young women, she urged them to return to their own homes because she could not provide for them.

We see the wisdom of Naomi in urging Orpah and Ruth to stay in Moab. She knew what it meant to be a foreigner in a strange land. She had gone through that experience when she came to Moab. She also knew if they stayed behind, she would be alone. But her love for them was greater than her need, and she desired their best. It must have been a sad sight that day on the road to Bethlehem as we see in Ruth 1:8, 14, 16–18:

> ⁸ And Naomi said unto her two daughters in law, Go, return each to her mother's house: the LORD deal kindly with you, as ye have dealt with the dead, and with me.
>
> ¹⁴ And they lifted up their voice, and wept again: and Orpah kissed her mother in law; but Ruth clave unto her.
>
> ¹⁶ And Ruth said, Intreat me not to leave thee, or to return from following after thee: for whither thou goest, I will go; and where thou lodgest, I will lodge: thy people shall be my people, and thy God my God:
>
> ¹⁷ Where thou diest, will I die, and there will I be buried: the LORD do so to me, and more also, if ought but death part thee and me.
>
> ¹⁸ When she saw that she was stedfastly minded to go with her, then she left speaking unto her.

Ruth 1:19–21 tells the events surrounding their return:

> ¹⁹ So they two went until they came to Bethlehem. And it came to pass, when they were come to Bethlehem, that all the city was moved about them, and they said, Is this Naomi?
>
> ²⁰ And she said unto them, Call me not Naomi, call me Mara: for the Almighty hath dealt very bitterly with me.

 [21] I went out full, and the LORD hath brought me home again empty: why then call ye me Naomi, seeing the LORD hath testified against me, and the Almighty hath afflicted me?

The people of Bethlehem were amazed at the difference in Naomi when she returned. Imagine how Ruth must have felt when she heard what was being said about her mother-in-law. Once again Naomi showed her wisdom. She admitted she was a different woman. She did not try to hide it. We do not read any words of criticism, only acknowledgment of the change that had taken place in her life.

Life in Bethlehem

Ruth and Naomi settled in Bethlehem. They were very poor. Ruth, being younger, went out to work in the fields. In return, Naomi gave her daughter-in-law wise counsel.

We will study more about Ruth in the next chapter. However, it was because of the beautiful relationship between Naomi and Ruth, as mother-in-law and daughter-in-law, that Naomi was able to lead Ruth in the proper steps to gain a husband according to Jewish law. This husband, Boaz, was related to Naomi's husband and could fulfill the family obligation toward Ruth.

Imagine the joy that came into Naomi's life when she became a grandmother! She thought she had lost all her family, but through Ruth and Boaz her life was once again full.

Ruth and Boaz named their son Obed. Obed had a son named Jesse who was the father of King David. Look at the genealogy in the first chapter of Matthew. We find Ruth, a Moabite woman, not only in the line from which David came, but also in the line from which Jesus the Messiah came.

Naomi is a beautiful example for women today. She was a loving and wise mother-in-law who cared for her daughters-in-law. I am sure that, as Naomi took care of her grandson, she passed on to him many truths about the God who had been so good to her.

CLOSING THOUGHTS

How is your relationship with your mother-in-law or daughter-in-law? If you are not married, what is your relationship with your mother? Do you live in love and open communication? Do you maintain a testimony of your personal faith in Jesus Christ as your Savior? As a believer in Jesus Christ, you should love others and show your love toward them. If love isn't there, ask God for healing and restoration in your family relationships. 1 John 4:7-8 speaks of this love:

> [7] Beloved, let us love one another: for love is of God; and every one that loveth is born of God, and knoweth God.
>
> [8] He that loveth not knoweth not God; for God is love.

FOR DISCUSSION

1. Describe two specific hardships Naomi faced.
2. Why did Naomi tell her daughters-in-law to return to Moab?
3. Why did Ruth and Naomi have such a close relationship?
4. What one quality in Naomi's life do you admire the most?
5. What joys came into Naomi's life?

CHAPTER 17

RUTH

A WOMAN WHO CHOSE WISELY: PART I

In the previous chapter, we studied the life of Naomi, a wise mother-in-law. In this study and the next one we will look at the life of Ruth, Naomi's daughter-in-law, to see the choices she made in her life.

Ruth's Marriage

An entire book in the Old Testament is devoted to the life of Ruth. Even more important, in the New Testament, Matthew lists Ruth in the genealogy of Jesus Christ. Let's ask God to help us learn from Ruth, so we, too, can make right choices. It seems we know how to make wrong choices without even trying!

We are not told if Elimelech chose brides for his sons before his death. The Bible simply says his sons took wives from Moab. In doing this, they directly disobeyed God's law against choosing a spouse from a heathen nation. Deuteronomy 7:3 says: *"Neither shalt thou make marriages with them; thy daughters thou shalt not give unto his son, nor his daughter shalt thou take unto thy son."*

The Bible tells us that Ruth became the bride of Mahlon, the first-born son of Naomi and her husband. We do not know how much influence this Jewish family had on Ruth. In Ruth 1:4, we read that Naomi's family lived in Moab for about ten years. That was long enough for Ruth to have heard and accepted all her husband and his family told her about the true and living God they worshiped.

Ruth's Widowhood

Ruth 1:3–5 explains that first Elimelech, Naomi's husband, died; then Mahlon, Ruth's husband, died. So Ruth became a young widow. This left her without any means of support. She became poor, a common condition for widows of that day. No one would have blamed her if she had become bitter or if she stayed with her own family in Moab.

Ruth did not do either. Instead, she decided to remain with her mother-in-law, Naomi. From the study about Naomi, we know that she, too, was a widow. Naomi, however, was a bitter woman. In spite of her bitterness, there was a bond of love between these two women. It drew Ruth to Naomi's side as they traveled back to Naomi's hometown of Bethlehem. We read Ruth's words to Naomi in Ruth 1:16–17:

> [16] And Ruth said, Intreat me not to leave thee, or to return from following after thee: for whither thou goest, I will go; and where thou lodgest, I will lodge: thy people shall be my people, and thy God my God:
> [17] Where thou diest, will I die, and there will I be buried: the LORD do so to me, and more also, if ought but death part thee and me.

Naomi had lost her husband and two sons, but she still had her two daughters-in-law, Orpah and Ruth. The three widows prepared to leave Moab to go to Naomi's people. When it came time to leave, however, Orpah went back to her heathen family and friends. With human reasoning, staying in Moab would seem the most logical choice. That makes Ruth's decision to stay with Naomi, even more surprising.

Ruth gives us a beautiful example of pure and unselfish devotion. Today, we see too many strained family relationships, broken homes, and loveless lives. It is refreshing to find this wonderful little story of love, right relationships, and right choices in God's Word.

Ruth Chooses the True God

Another right choice Ruth made was to serve the true and living God. In spite of her heathen background, she became a devout worshiper of the true God. Just when, how, or under what circumstances this happened, we are not told. However, on the road to Bethlehem, she showed evidence of her faith in God. She made a firm decision to follow Jehovah and identified completely with His people by saying to Naomi, *"Your people shall be my people, and your God, my God"* (Ruth 1:16). Here we can ask ourselves: *"Have I made the right choice to serve the true and living God? Have I made that choice evident to those I love?"*

Making Important Decisions

Ruth made wise choices in the direction of her life and in turning to the true God. She made other right choices that we will study in the next lesson. First, however, let us look at what God says about making right decisions.

Relying Upon God

Sometimes it is hard to have enough confidence in ourselves to know we have made the right choice. The very first thing we *must* know is that there is a true and living God, and we can know Him personally.

Who is the true God? Moses was faced with convincing the Israelites that God had indeed sent him to deliver them from bondage in Egypt. Moses asked God what he should say to convince them. God told Moses exactly what to say. We read this in Exodus 3:14, *"And God said unto Moses, I am that I am. Thus shalt thou say unto the children of Israel, I am hath sent me unto you."* The verse teaches that God exists in and of Himself without needing any other being to sustain Him.

I find it strengthening to my faith to know that God does not have to prove His power or abilities; He simply says, "I AM!" He is God because He is God. He does not need to give any reason, giving confidence in His presence that can never be taken away or doubted.

CLOSING THOUGHTS

When we choose to have a personal relationship with the true God, all other decisions can be answered through prayer, seeking His counsel through His Word and through the circumstances and people in our lives. It is logical that we must spend time with God and His Word if we want to come to know Him and His will more fully. That is the way we can have confidence in Him and in our decisions.

Psalm 1:1–4 speaks of the person who diligently seeks God:

¹ Blessed is the man that walketh not in the counsel of the ungodly, nor standeth in the way of sinners, nor sitteth in the seat of the scornful.

² But his delight is in the law of the LORD; and in his law doth he meditate day and night.

³ And he shall be like a tree planted by the rivers of water, that bringeth forth his fruit in his season; his leaf also shall not wither; and whatsoever he doeth shall prosper.

⁴ The ungodly are not so: but are like the chaff which the wind driveth away.

Notice the difference. One person is prosperous; the other is like the worthless chaff of grain that the wind blows away. The difference is the time spent with God in prayer and making decisions based on obedience to His Word.

Ruth was an example of a person whom God blessed. She chose to spend time with the right people, joining herself to her mother-in-law and the people of God. Her most important decision, however, was the decision to serve the true God according to the laws written in His Word. In the next chapter we will see more about her obedience to God's Word after she arrived in Judah.

Think for a moment about yourself. Are you facing decisions, big or small? Accept these decisions as an opportunity to make right choices. The most important decision to make is to serve the true and living God. All you have to do is ask Him to reveal Himself to you and be willing to accept what He shows you about Himself in His Word. Jesus paid for your sin by dying on the cross; accept that payment for yourself. Then depend upon Him to help you with the other decisions you must make.

In the book of Psalms we find verses that speak of God's willingness to teach and guide us when we look to Him.

- *"I will instruct thee and teach thee in the way which thou shalt go: I will guide thee with mine eye"* (Psalm 32:8).
- *"The steps of a good man are ordered by the LORD: and he delighteth in his way. Though he fall, he shall not be utterly cast down: for the LORD upholdeth him with his hand"* (Psalm 37:23-24).
- *"Thy Word is a lamp unto my feet, and a light unto my path"* (Psalm 119:105).

FOR DISCUSSION

1. What made Ruth's decision to stay with Naomi so unusual?
2. Name three difficulties that came into Ruth's life.
3. What decision or choices are you facing in your life?
4. What is the most important decision you will ever make?
5. List three methods to help make wise decisions.

CHAPTER 18

RUTH

A WOMAN WHO CHOSE WISELY: PART 2

When we looked at the first part of Ruth's life, we saw how she chose the right family, the true and living God, and the right people. Continuing our study, we will see three more right choices she made: the right field, the right advice, and the right timing.

God's Instructions

When Ruth and Naomi returned to Bethlehem, they were widows without any means to support themselves. However, in Old Testament law, God provided a way for widows to get food. God gave His instructions to landowners in Deuteronomy 24:19: *"When thou cuttest down thine harvest in thy field, and hast forgot a sheaf in the field, thou shalt not go again to fetch it: it shall be for the stranger, for the fatherless, and for the widow: that the LORD thy God may bless thee in all the work of thine hands."*

Naomi must have taught Ruth the laws of God, because Ruth knew about this law. Ruth asked Naomi to let her go and gather the grain that fell behind the reapers. Naomi gave her permission, and Ruth went to work. She went to a field belonging to a man named Boaz, a member of her father-in-law's family.

Ruth 2:5–6, 8, 10–12:

⁵ Then said Boaz unto his servant that was set over the reapers, Whose damsel is this?

⁶ And the servant that was set over the reapers

answered and said, It is the Moabitish damsel that came
back with Naomi out of the country of Moab:

⁸ Then said Boaz unto Ruth, Hearest thou not, my
daughter? Go not to glean in another field, neither go
from hence, but abide here fast by my maidens:

¹⁰ Then she fell on her face, and bowed herself to the
ground, and said unto him, Why have I found grace in
thine eyes, that thou shouldest take knowledge of me,
seeing I am a stranger?

¹¹ And Boaz answered and said unto her, It hath fully
been shewed me, all that thou hast done unto thy
mother in law since the death of thine husband: and
how thou hast left thy father and thy mother, and the
land of thy nativity, and art come unto a people which
thou knewest not heretofore.

¹² The LORD recompense thy work, and a full
reward be given thee of the LORD God of Israel,
under whose wings thou art come to trust.

God's Provision

This is a wonderful story of God's provision for Ruth and
Naomi by leading Ruth to the field of a relative of her husband.
Ruth was an example of humility when she bowed before Boaz.
He recognized her and praised her for her loyalty to Naomi. The
way we treat people and the choices we make are a testimony to
others—either for good or for bad.

The story does not end there. Boaz told Ruth to glean only
in his field, and also told her to eat and drink with his workers.
He left enough food for her to be able to take some to Naomi.
Then he told the workers to drop extra grain for Ruth to
pick up.

How excited Ruth must have been that first night when she
got home and told Naomi all that had happened. Of course,
Naomi was thrilled. She asked the name of the man who had

shown Ruth such kindness. Ruth told her mother-in-law that the man's name was Boaz. The story continues in Ruth 2:20–23:

> [20] And Naomi said unto her daughter in law, Blessed be he of the LORD, who hath not left off his kindness to the living and to the dead. And Naomi said unto her, The man is near of kin unto us, one of our next kinsmen.
>
> [22] And Naomi said unto Ruth her daughter in law, It is good, my daughter, that thou go out with his maidens, that they meet thee not in any other field.
>
> [23] So she kept fast by the maidens of Boaz to glean unto the end of barley harvest and of wheat harvest; and dwelt with her mother in law.

As Ruth told her mother-in-law what had happened, Naomi was encouraged to see the Lord's hand of blessing in her life again. She quickly gave God the praise due Him. Each of us needs to be careful to thank God for His goodness in our lives.

Ruth's Future

Naomi carefully and wisely told Ruth the steps she should take to secure a husband who could provide for her for the rest of her life. The husband she was to seek was Boaz.

Throughout the rest of the story, we see how Ruth followed her mother-in-law's advice step by step. She really didn't have to; after all, she was a grown woman. She had already been married and lived a life of her own. The love, devotion, and respect between these two godly women led Ruth to make the right choice—to follow Naomi's advice.

This love story from God's Word is for all people everywhere. The story shows the result of following the right advice and waiting for the right time. The story brings Ruth to the time and place for Boaz to be able to redeem her. Redemption, meaning to buy back, was the Old Testament way of continuing the family line.

Conflict now enters the picture. Boaz was not the first in line to redeem Ruth. Scripture tells us Boaz went to the man who was the closest relative, telling him of the situation. According to custom, the two met before the elders of the city. The closest relative was unable to redeem the possessions of Elimelech and his sons. Thus, he turned his right to do so over to Boaz, who was able to redeem them so that Ruth could become his wife.

Ruth followed the advice given to her even though the customs of her own people were different. Only because of Naomi's knowledge of God's Word was she able to give wise counsel to Ruth. When we either give or receive advice, we should be careful to make sure it agrees with God's Word. In order to be able to do that, we must know the Bible well. Then, as we follow it, we will make the right choices for ourselves and be able to help others.

I am sure Ruth must have wondered what was going to happen as she approached Boaz. She certainly appreciated his kindness, and since he was an older man, she no doubt respected him. At the same time, she must have had fears about how everything would turn out. Maybe she even wondered if she was doing the right thing. Despite her feelings, she followed the advice Naomi gave her.

God blessed the marriage of Ruth and Boaz, giving them a son whom they named Obed. In Matthew, when we read the genealogy of the Messiah, we find Boaz, Ruth, and Obed. What an honor was given to Ruth, the Moabitess. Indeed, she was a woman who knew how to make right choices.

CLOSING THOUGHTS

The God-given principle of redemption is still in effect today in a personal way. Jesus Christ redeemed us by paying the price for our sin. Romans 6:23 says: *"For the wages of sin is death; but the gift of God is eternal life through Jesus Christ our Lord."*

As Ruth had to accept the redemption offered by Boaz, so each of us must accept the redemption offered by God in order for it to benefit us. Have you done this? If not, admit you are a sinner and cannot pay for your sin by yourself. Believe that Jesus died for your sin, and accept Him as your sacrifice and Savior.

FOR DISCUSSION

1. How did Ruth know to go behind the reapers to gather grain?
2. Name two characteristics Ruth showed in her relationship with Boaz and Naomi.
3. List three characteristics of Boaz.
4. In what way did Naomi's life change after she left Moab?
5. In your own words, describe the relationship between Ruth and Naomi.

CHAPTER 19

HANNAH

A PRAYING WOMAN

Hannah is remembered as a woman of prayer. What is prayer? It is communication between a person and God. Prayer may be out loud or silent. Prayer includes listening to God, praising Him for who He is and what He has done, asking forgiveness for our sins, and making requests for ourselves and for others. In prayer we express feelings such as grief, frustration, disappointment, or joy, delight, and thanks. Prayer is simply sharing anything and everything with God. Prayer presumes we have faith in God as we talk with Him.

We can read about prayer and can learn much from the prayers of others, but the most important thing is to pray. When we go to God in prayer, we see Him respond, and He becomes real to us. Hannah found that to be true in her own life.

Hannah: The Woman and Wife

Hannah was the mother of the prophet Samuel. She is one of the most well-known women in the Bible because of her prayer to God asking for a son.

Hannah was one of Elkanah's wives. The other one, Peninnah, had several children, but Hannah had none. Peninnah made life unhappy for Hannah by constantly reminding her that she gave no children to Elkanah.

Yet the Bible tells us that Elkanah loved Hannah and favored her over Peninnah. From their story in the first chapter of 1 Samuel, we find that Elkanah and Hannah were a husband and wife who loved and feared God. They knew it was necessary to have a personal relationship with God in order for their prayers to be heard.

Today, our personal relationship with God comes through faith in Jesus Christ who died on the Cross to pay for our sins. 1 Timothy 2:5 tells us: *"For there is one God, and one mediator between God and men, the man Christ Jesus."*

Each year Elkanah and his wives traveled from the hill country where they lived to the city of Shiloh to offer sacrifices according to Old Testament law. While on these trips, Peninnah harassed Hannah. However, Elkanah loved Hannah. Because she had no children, he gave her a double portion of the festive meal that followed the sacrifice. This went on year after year.

Hannah lived under a lot of pressure. Some of us experience pressure, too. How we cope with pressure is the important thing. The Bible never says that Hannah tried to get even with Peninnah. Nothing indicates that Hannah was angry with her husband for having another wife. We find no record that she blamed God or was angry with Him for her childless condition. She continued with her responsibilities as a wife. However, because she wept and wouldn't eat, her husband knew she was unhappy and asked her: *"Am not I better to thee than ten sons?"* (1 Samuel 1:8).

Hannah's Prayer of Faith

What did Hannah do in her heartbroken state? She opened her heart in silent prayer to God. Words could not express her deepest feelings, but she still prayed. And then, as if she were not hurting enough, Eli, the priest, misunderstood her actions and accused her of being drunk. We read the story in 1 Samuel 1:12–18:

> [12] And it came to pass, as she continued praying before the LORD, that Eli marked her mouth.
> [13] Now Hannah, she spake in her heart; only her lips

moved, but her voice was not heard: therefore Eli thought she had been drunken.

¹⁴ And Eli said unto her, How long wilt thou be drunken? put away thy wine from thee.

¹⁵ And Hannah answered and said, No, my lord, I am a woman of a sorrowful spirit: I have drunk neither wine nor strong drink, but have poured out my soul before the LORD.

¹⁶ Count not thine handmaid for a daughter of Belial: for out of the abundance of my complaint and grief have I spoken hitherto.

¹⁷ Then Eli answered and said, Go in peace: and the God of Israel grant thee thy petition that thou hast asked of him.

¹⁸ And she said, Let thine handmaid find grace in thy sight. So the woman went her way, and did eat, and her countenance was no more sad.

Hannah is an example of faith. After she prayed, she believed. She trusted God so strongly that she completely changed. She was no longer sad. Do we pray with that kind of faith? Even though we pray, we often keep on worrying.

Jesus told his disciples in Matthew 6:30–33: *"Wherefore, if God so clothe the grass of the field, which today is, and tomorrow is cast into the oven, shall he not much more clothe you, 0 ye of little faith? Therefore take no thought, saying, What shall we eat? or, What shall we drink? or, Wherewithal shall we be clothed? (For after all these things do the Gentiles seek:) for your heavenly Father knoweth that ye have need of all these things. But seek ye first the kingdom of God, and his righteousness; and all these things shall be added unto you."*

God answered Hannah's prayer! She conceived and gave birth to a son. She called his name Samuel, which means "heard of God" (1 Samuel 1:20). Each time Hannah spoke her son's name, she was reminded of what God had done for her.

Hannah Keeps Her Promise

Hannah made a promise to the Lord to return her son to Him. After he was born, she kept Samuel until he was weaned, probably about three years. Then she returned to the house of God and left her son with Eli, the priest, where the little boy was to work for the Lord. Here are Hannah's words as she spoke to Eli in 1 Samuel 1:26–28:

> [26] And she said, Oh my lord, as thy soul liveth, my lord, I am the woman that stood by thee here, praying unto the LORD.
>
> [27] For this child I prayed; and the LORD hath given me my petition which I asked of him:
>
> [28] Therefore also I have lent him to the LORD; as long as he liveth he shall be lent to the LORD. And he worshipped the LORD there.

Once again, look at Hannah's faith. She completely trusted God to care for her child. You can imagine how hard it was to leave Samuel. The Bible tells us Hannah saw him only once each year when she went to the house of God to worship. Each time, she brought Samuel a new coat she had made for him. After the visit, she had to leave him again. But she kept her promise to God. The Lord rewarded Hannah with three more sons and two daughters (1 Samuel 2:21).

Lessons from Hannah's Life

What can we learn from Hannah? One thing we see is the value of dedicating our children to God. Think of all the time Hannah must have spent tenderly teaching Samuel during his early childhood. She probably taught him about God, about the value of prayer, how he was an answer to prayer, and how he was born to serve the Lord. We need to ask God to help us be a godly influence in the lives of our children.

Here is another lesson from the story of Hannah. We cannot underestimate the hurt and damage our words can do to others.

Often we are quick to say unkind words, or speak thoughtlessly. Peninnah's words gave Hannah much heartache. James 3:5 says: *"Even so the tongue is a little member, and boasteth great things. Behold, how great a matter a little fire kindleth!"*

Hannah was also misunderstood by Eli, the priest. It is easy to misjudge someone because of his actions. Hannah showed us how to defend ourselves with humility. She didn't get angry. With respect for Eli's position, she simply explained how she felt and what her motives were.

CLOSING THOUGHTS

Hannah is a wonderful example of a woman who trusted God with her problem. She also was a godly mother who prayed for her son and yielded him totally to God. She experienced the trust of Psalm 34:19: *"Many are the afflictions of the righteous: but the LORD delivereth him out of them all."*

FOR DISCUSSION

1. Name three ways in which Hannah was a godly example of how to live under pressure.
2. List three words that describe Hannah's prayer.
3. How would you describe your own prayer life?
4. Do you remember a time when someone's words hurt you? How did you react?
5. How was Hannah a godly example as a mother?

CHAPTER 20

MICHAL

DAVID'S FIRST WIFE

After the times of the judges, the people of Israel demanded a king, even though that was not God's plan for them. The first king of Israel was Saul.

King Saul was Michal's father. Her brother, Jonathan, was David's best friend. Perhaps she had seen David when he visited Jonathan.

Michal's Marriage to David

Michal's older sister, Merab, had been promised by King Saul as a wife to David to reward him for fighting the Philistines. The Bible says King Saul changed his mind when it was time to give Merab away. 1 Samuel 18:14–15, 17, 19 gives the account:

[14] And David behaved himself wisely in all his ways; and the LORD was with him.

[15] Wherefore when Saul saw that he behaved himself very wisely, he was afraid of him.

[17] And Saul said to David, Behold my elder daughter Merab, her will I give thee to wife: only be thou valiant for me, and fight the LORD'S battles. For Saul said, Let not mine hand be upon him, but let the hand of the Philistines be upon him.

[19] But it came to pass at the time when Merab Saul's daughter should have been given to David, that she was given unto Adriel the Meholathite to wife.

The Israelites were pleased with David because of his valiant deeds, and they sang his praises. Seeing this, King Saul grew jealous of David. His jealousy caused much harm for everyone. He tried to murder David several times. Saul tried to kill David when he realized his daughter Michal loved David. He plotted against David by setting as his dowry the foreskins of 100 Philistines. Saul thought certainly David would be killed by the Philistines in that effort.

1 Samuel 18:20–21, 25, 27, 29 continues the story:

²⁰ And Michal Saul's daughter loved David: and they told Saul, and the thing pleased him.

²¹ And Saul said, I will give him her, that she may be a snare to him, and that the hand of the Philistines may be against him. Wherefore Saul said to David, Thou shalt this day be my son in law in the one of the twain.

²⁵ And Saul said, Thus shall ye say to David, The king desireth not any dowry, but an hundred foreskins of the Philistines, to be avenged of the king's enemies. But Saul thought to make David fall by the hand of the Philistines.

²⁷ Wherefore David arose and went, he and his men, and slew of the Philistines two hundred men; and David brought their foreskins, and they gave them in full tale to the king, that he might be the king's son in law. And Saul gave him Michal his daughter to wife.

²⁹ And Saul was yet the more afraid of David; and Saul became David's enemy continually.

Michal Saves David's Life

King Saul continued to plot against David. The Bible does not say how Michal reacted to her father's hatred of the husband whom she loved, but her father's jealousy of her husband put Michal in a difficult situation. Her scheme to save her husband's life shows how she felt toward David, as we read in 1 Samuel 19:10–12:

> [10] And Saul sought to smite David even to the wall
> with the javelin; but he slipped away out of Saul's pres-
> ence, and he smote the javelin into the wall: and David
> fled, and escaped that night.
> [11] Saul also sent messengers unto David's house, to
> watch him, and to slay him in the morning: and Michal
> David's wife told him, saying, If thou save not thy life
> to night, to morrow thou shalt be slain.
> [12] So Michal let David down through a window: and
> he went, and fled, and escaped.

David escaped from King Saul with Michal's help. Her father
demanded that David come to see him, but Michal made a
dummy, put it in the bed, and told the king David was sick. So
Saul told his servants to bring the bed with David in it. Imagine
how angry the king was when he found out he had been tricked
again.

Under normal circumstances it is wrong to disobey your
father or resist legitimate authority. In this case, however, Michal
showed daring defiance of a father who had become insane with
hatred of David. She displayed courage in saving her husband's
life. Even so, as we read on in 1 Samuel, David was forced to live
like an outlaw in exile.

Michal Given to Another Man

With David out of his way—at least for a while—King Saul
arranged for Michal to marry a man named Paltiel. When David
returned and became king, he demanded Michal be returned to
him. 2 Samuel 3:15–16 tells us that Paltiel wept as Michal was
taken away.

Michal Despised David

After David became king, he brought the ark of the covenant
back to Jerusalem. He chose 30,000 men of Israel to carry the

ark. As they marched into Jerusalem, David became so happy he danced for joy. 2 Samuel 6:14–17, 20–23 reveals Michal's reaction to this spectacle:

> [14] And David danced before the LORD with all his might; and David was girded with a linen ephod.
>
> [15] So David and all the house of Israel brought up the ark of the LORD with shouting, and with the sound of the trumpet.
>
> [16] And as the ark of the LORD came into the city of David, Michal Saul's daughter looked through a window, and saw king David leaping and dancing before the LORD; and she despised him in her heart.
>
> [17] And they brought in the ark of the LORD, and set it in his place, in the midst of the tabernacle that David had pitched for it: and David offered burnt offerings and peace offerings before the LORD.
>
> [20] Then David returned to bless his household. And Michal the daughter of Saul came out to meet David, and said, How glorious was the king of Israel to day, who uncovered himself to day in the eyes of the handmaids of his servants, as one of the vain fellows shamelessly uncovereth himself!
>
> [21] And David said unto Michal, It was before the LORD, which chose me before thy father, and before all his house, to appoint me ruler over the people of the LORD, over Israel: therefore will I play before the LORD.
>
> [22] And I will yet be more vile than thus, and will be base in mine own sight: and of the maidservants which thou hast spoken of, of them shall I be had in honour.
>
> [23] Therefore Michal the daughter of Saul had no child unto the day of her death.

These verses show us Michal's resentment. Perhaps she did not understand the significance of the ark of the covenant or David's zeal for the Lord. Whatever Michal's relationship to the Lord, she should not have rebuked her husband publicly for his actions. The Bible says that, in the end, she had no children.

What a contrast between Michal when we first met her and years later. She started out deeply loving David, and ended up despising him in her heart.

What went wrong? What can we learn from Michal? The most obvious lesson is the disharmony, unhappiness, and tragedy that comes when a couple does not worship the one true God together. Families and teachers need to help young people understand this important principle.

Michal's initial love for David was not enough to ensure a happy marriage. Often people want to get married despite different beliefs. They imagine their love for each other will hold their marriage together. It doesn't work that way.

Also Michal did not understand, nor even try to understand, her husband's actions. She judged him to be wrong and she publicly rebuked him. Even when David explained, Michal failed to ask forgiveness. So often we wrongly judge people because we misunderstand their motives.

CLOSING THOUGHTS

True God-given love between a man and a woman brings harmony and understanding. A Christian home should be a happy and secure place where husbands truly love their wives and wives sincerely respect their husbands. What is the situation in your home?

FOR DISCUSSION

1. How did David and Michal become husband and wife?
2. In what ways did they show their love for one another?

3. Why wasn't their love strong enough to keep their home happy?
4. What do you think God wants us to learn from this story?
5. Describe your home situation in terms of love, respect, and commitment to God and each other.

CHAPTER 21

ABIGAIL

A WOMAN OF PEACE

The Bible gives many examples of family life, but few of them are what we would call "ideal" situations. Some were families with multiple wives, or wives who were childless. Others had disobedient children, financial problems, sickness, death, or a husband and wife who didn't share a common faith. Since so many of these problems are similar to the ones in our homes, we sometimes think of these situations as "normal." But we should not accept as normal things we can change for the better with God's help.

God is good in giving us examples of women who lived in "real life" home situations. We can see how, with God's help, they maintained relatively peaceful homes in spite of their problems. Abigail was just such a woman.

Abigail's Background

The story takes place after David was anointed as God's choice for the next king of Israel. King Saul, however, was still on the throne and more jealous of David than ever. The king was still trying to kill David.

David and his men roamed the countryside providing protection for farmers. In exchange, the farmers gave food to them and their animals. One of the men who received protection was a wealthy man named Nabal, Abigail's husband. During the sheep-shearing season, David sent his men to Nabal and asked for food, but Nabal refused to give it to them.

Abigail's Circumstances

1 Samuel 25:2–3 gives insight into Nabal and Abigail's home life:

> ² And there was a man in Maon, whose possessions were in Carmel; and the man was very great, and he had three thousand sheep, and a thousand goats: and he was shearing his sheep in Carmel.
>
> ³ Now the name of the man was Nabal; and the name of his wife Abigail: and she was a woman of good understanding, and of a beautiful countenance: but the man was churlish and evil in his doings.

Nabal is described as harsh, rude, and brutal. He was rich and was often drunk. From other verses we know he worshiped a false god. Nabal's name means "a fool." As we read this story, we can see how well his name described him.

Abigail, however, is described as intelligent and beautiful. Often women are caught up in trying to look beautiful, but neglect their minds. Surely, a beautiful woman who has good understanding is one of God's masterpieces.

Abigail and David

David and his men had been good to Nabal. So David sent ten of his men with a greeting of peace and told them to ask Nabal for what was owed them. When Nabal refused to give them food, David decided to kill Nabal and his household. One of Nabal's servants heard of this and told Abigail, pleading with her to do something. Notice that the servant came to her rather than to his master. Abigail acted immediately. Without telling her husband, she took as much food as she thought David and his men might need and personally went to deliver it to David.

Just when David's anger was at its peak, Abigail met him, fell at his feet and presented him with the food. She was humble, accepted the blame for her husband's actions, and explained that foolishness was part of his nature. She acknowledged that David's men had been good protectors and asked him to spare the life of her husband and their household.

Abigail could have been tempted to let David kill Nabal, which would have legally freed her from her miserable marriage. Imagine how often she must have been placed in the position of excusing Nabal's behavior. Yet she remained faithful. 1 Peter 3:1, 5 speaks about relationships between husbands and wives: *"Likewise, ye wives, be in subjection to your own husbands; that, if any obey not the word, they also may without the word be won by the conversation of the wives; For after this manner in the old time the holy women also, who trusted in God, adorned themselves, being in subjection unto their own husbands."*

Abigail's peace offering and her calmness soothed David's anger. She did not rebuke him; instead she spoke wisely and kindly. She reminded David he was God's choice of king, and he should not react out of anger. She knew it was God's place to take revenge. David remembered that, too, once he calmed down.

Lessons from Abigail's Life

Even though Abigail was married to a harsh, drunken fool, she did not become bitter. She was not a nag, full of self-pity, or hatred. She accepted her circumstances and graciously upheld her duties.

The timing of Abigail's intervention is one of the lessons we can learn from her. When we have wisdom to share, courage to act, and help to offer, we should not hesitate to act, regardless of the risks involved. Abigail's peace mission was successful. She returned home to her wicked husband and resumed her hard life. She did not try to leave Nabal or get a divorce. She had made her vows "for better or for worse." Her life was certainly "worse."

God's Solution

Abigail's story continues in 1 Samuel 25:36–38:

> ³⁶ And Abigail came to Nabal; and, behold, he held a feast in his house, like the feast of a king; and Nabal's heart was merry within him for he was very drunken: wherefore she told him nothing, less or more, until the morning light.
>
> ³⁷ But it came to pass in the morning, when the wine was gone out of Nabal, and his wife had told him these things, that his heart died within him, and he became as a stone.
>
> ³⁸ And it came to pass about ten days after, that the Lord smote Nabal, that he died.

Abigail showed tremendous character and faith in the way she trusted God's timing in her husband's life. The Bible never tells of attempts on Abigail's part to change Nabal, nor does it tell us of any time when Abigail tried to get out of her marriage. She suffered because of her husband's behavior, but she stayed firm in her role as Nabal's wife, always working to keep peace.

When David heard of Nabal's death, he took Abigail as his wife. God does not promise he will always remove our problems, but He does promise to be with us *in* our problems. God's solution to Abigail's difficult home life came in His time and His way. Possibly Abigail felt some sense of loss for the man to whom she had been so loyal, but she accepted God's sovereignty.

CLOSING THOUGHTS

Abigail was a woman of peace. Peace can be described in various ways. At the time of salvation, believers receive peace *with* God. *"Therefore being justified by faith, we have peace with God through our Lord Jesus Christ"* (Romans 5:1).

Throughout our daily lives, believers can experience the peace *of* God. *"Be careful for nothing; but in every thing by prayer and supplication with thanksgiving let your requests be made known unto God. And the peace of God which passeth all understanding, shall keep your hearts and minds through Christ Jesus"* (Philippians 4:7).

Peace of mind—the ability to go to sleep at night without worry—is a witness to those around us that the Prince of Peace lives and works within us.

Just before Jesus left this earth He said to His disciples: *"Peace I leave with you, my peace I give unto you: not as the world giveth, give I unto you. Let not your heart be troubled, neither let it be afraid"* (John 14:27).

Do you have peace in your life? Is your home a peaceful place? Do you try to make and keep peace in your family? Do other people think of you as a peacemaker?

How can you—like Abigail—be a woman of peace? God gives the answer in Isaiah 26:3–4: *"Thou wilt keep him in perfect peace, whose mind is stayed on thee: because he trusteth in thee. Trust ye in the Lord forever: for in the Lord Jehovah is everlasting strength."*

FOR DISCUSSION

1. Describe Abigail's marriage.
2. List the ways Abigail displayed the godliness spoken about in 1 Peter 3:1–6.
3. Name three of Abigail's personality traits.
4. Which ones did she demonstrate in her moment of crisis?
5. How can *you* be a woman of peace?

CHAPTER 22

BATHSHEBA

MOTHER OF KING SOLOMON

Israel was at war, but King David did not lead his men into battle as he should have. By this time, David had ruled as king for 12 years and decided to stay home rather than go to war. Because King David was not where he should have been, he entered into sin.

Bathsheba was the wife of Uriah, a Hittite, a loyal soldier in King David's army. Uriah was fighting for Israel. The true account is told in 2 Samuel 11:1–5:

> [1] David tarried still at Jerusalem.
>
> [2] And it came to pass in an eveningtide, that David arose from off his bed, and walked upon the roof of the king's house: and from the roof he saw a woman washing herself; and the woman was very beautiful to look upon.
>
> [3] And David sent and enquired after the woman. And one said, Is not this Bathsheba, the daughter of Eliam, the wife of Uriah the Hittite?
>
> [4] And David sent messengers, and took her; and she came in unto him, and he lay with her; for she was purified from her uncleanness: and she returned unto her house.
>
> [5] And the woman conceived, and sent and told David, and said, I am with child.

Let's think carefully about what we have read. David was in Jerusalem rather than at the battlefront. Bathsheba was bathing on her roof. Most roofs in Eastern countries are flat, and often activities such as eating, visiting, and sleeping take place on the roofs. But most people do *not* bathe in public on their roofs. David was up on his roof, too. His was probably higher than Bathsheba's because he lived in the palace. From his vantage point, he looked down and saw her. She was beautiful and even though David learned she was married, he sent for her and engaged in adultery.

Bathsheba's Responsibility

When David was confronted with his sin, he took all the blame. But didn't Bathsheba also bear some responsibility? Why was she bathing in public in the first place? She did not show any modesty by being uncovered on a rooftop where she could be observed by people in other houses.

If Bathsheba had been a faithful wife and a woman of strong conviction, perhaps she and David would never have this stain of sin on their record. But since it did happen and is recorded in Scripture, let's see what God wants to teach us about the consequences of sin.

David's Reaction

When David learned Bathsheba was pregnant, he thought of a plot to hide their sin. He called her husband, Uriah, home from the war. David assumed he would sleep with his wife. Then when it became known she was pregnant, it would seem like a normal result of her husband's visit. It seemed like a good idea, but 2 Samuel 11:9–11 tells what actually happened:

> [9] But Uriah slept at the door of the king's house with all the servants of his lord, and went not down to his house.
>
> [10] And when they had told David, saying, Uriah went not down unto his house, David said unto Uriah,

Camest thou not from thy journey? why then didst
thou not go down unto thine house?

¹¹ And Uriah said unto David, The ark, and Israel, and
Judah, abide in tents; and my lord Joab, and the servants
of my lord, are encamped in the open fields; shall I
then go into mine house, to eat and to drink, and to
lie with my wife? as thou livest, and as thy soul liveth,
I will not do this thing.

Again, the question could be asked about Bathsheba's responsibility. The Bible tells us her husband slept at the door
rather than with his wife. Certainly Bathsheba knew Uriah was
there. It does not appear that Bathsheba went to see him or in
any way told him what she and King David had done or that she
was pregnant. She did not own up to what had taken place while
Uriah was away at the battle.

David's scheme didn't work because Uriah was a loyal soldier. He would not enjoy the pleasures of his home while fellow
soldiers were out on the battlefield. David then had to devise
another plot. He sent word to the captain of the army commanding that Uriah be placed in the front line of battle. The
other soldiers were ordered to withdraw leaving Uriah to be
killed. This evil plan worked, and Uriah died in battle. David
went from one evil act to another. First he committed adultery,
then murder to try to hide it.

The Consequences

2 Samuel 11:26–27 continues the account:.

²⁶ And when the wife of Uriah heard that Uriah her
husband was dead, she mourned for her husband.

²⁷ And when the mourning was past, David sent and
fetched her to his house, and she became his wife, and
bare him a son. But the thing that David had done
displeased the LORD.

Now it was all over, David had what he wanted; Bathsheba was his wife. The baby was born and there did not seem to be any public disgrace. But God sent the prophet Nathan to confront David. Nathan heard David's confession of his great sin and assured him the Lord had forgiven him. Nathan also told David that the child would die. True to the prophecy, the baby died seven days later.

David and Bathsheba's grief and sorrow over the death of this child must have been intense. Undoubtedly, the death of their son made them both deeply aware of the consequences of their sin. However, God has used their sorrow to help others whose loss has nothing to do with sin. Words can never erase pain or the sense of loss during a time of grief, but in this story we find words which have brought comfort to many people whose babies and young children have died. David said, *"But now he is dead, wherefore should I fast? can I bring him back again? I shall go to him, but he shall not return to me."* (2 Samuel 12:23). David knew he would see his child again in the Resurrection.

Physical death is not the end of existence; there is life after death, of that we can be sure. Those of us who have trusted Jesus Christ as Savior and accepted His payment for sin on our behalf can have the same assurance David had that we will see our loved ones again.

Bathsheba's Reaction

What was Bathsheba's reaction to her child's death? Did she shed tears of repentance? Apparently she did, because the Bible says that David comforted her, and she conceived and bore another son who was named Solomon, which means "peaceable." He could have been born to any of David's wives, but he was given to Bathsheba.

King Solomon succeeded David as ruler over all Israel. Solomon was a wise king. We don't read much more about Bathsheba, but we can imagine she carefully raised and taught her son in the ways of the Lord. We can see the evidence of his good upbringing in the book of Proverbs. He gives wise counsel on how to raise children. He also says much about the ways of a man with a woman.

Bathsheba is referred to in Matthew's genealogy of the Messiah. Matthew 1:6 says, *"And Jesse begat David the king; and David the king begat Solomon of her that had been the wife of Urias."*

God forgave both David and Bathsheba, but notice how her name is listed in the genealogy. Bathsheba is remembered as having been Uriah's wife, not David's.

CLOSING THOUGHTS

Bathsheba accepted God's forgiveness and did not let one sin ruin her entire life. She learned from her mistake and went on to raise a family.

It is sometimes hard to believe and accept God's forgiveness and to forgive ourselves. Women especially seem to brood and mull over the past. In doing so, we rob ourselves of spiritual growth. In addition, we are miserable and unhappy. Often, we have low self-esteem and bear burdens of guilt we were never meant to carry.

We need to learn from David and Bathsheba how to be happy in God's forgiveness. In Psalm 32:1, 2, we read David's words written after he had confessed his sins and experienced God's forgiveness: *"Blessed is he whose transgression is forgiven, whose sin is covered. Blessed is the man unto whom the LORD imputeth not iniquity, and in whose spirit there is no guile."*

Don't ruin your life by living with a load of sin and guilt. With a humble spirit, ask God to forgive your sins. Be specific as you pray, not a general, *"If* I have sinned, please forgive me." Rather, before you go to sleep, think back over the day. Ask yourself if you have sinned in your actions, your words, your attitudes, or your thoughts. Mention those by name to God and ask for His forgiveness. Ask God to help you remember any sins you may

have forgotten or overlooked. Then claim God's promise found
in 1 John 1:9, *"If we confess our sins, He is faithful and just to forgive
us our sins and to cleanse us from all unrighteousness."*

FOR DISCUSSION

1. What were the circumstances surrounding the first time
   David saw Bathsheba?
2. What responsibility did Bathsheba have in this incident?
3. David plotted twice to cover up the sin. How and why did
   David's schemes fail?
4. What consequences did David and Bathsheba endure?
5. What can we learn about God's forgiveness from this story?

CHAPTER 23

TWO HARLOT MOTHERS

REVEALING THE TRUE MOTHER'S LOVE

Women often face situations that demand wisdom beyond what we have. We need God's wisdom to helps us understand other people correctly.

God Grants King Solomon Wisdom

This account gives perhaps the Bible's most vivid example of how God can and does give wisdom. In the book of 1 Kings, we are told that when Solomon became king, he feared God and served Him. God was pleased and told Solomon He would grant him anything he desired. The conversation between God and the young King Solomon is told in 1 Kings 3:5, 9–10:

> [5] In Gibeon the LORD appeared to Solomon in a dream by night: and God said, Ask what I shall give thee.
> [9] Give therefore thy servant an understanding heart to judge thy people, that I may discern between good and bad: for who is able to judge this thy so great a people?
> [10] And the speech pleased the Lord, that Solomon had asked this thing.

The Bible says Solomon asked God for an understanding heart in order to have discernment. That is true wisdom. God was so pleased with Solomon's request that He not only granted Solomon wisdom, He also gave him great riches.

Two Women Appeal to the King

In 1 Kings 3:16–22, following the discussion between God and Solomon, we find the story of the two harlot mothers who are the subject of this study.

[16] Then came there two women, that were harlots, unto the king, and stood before him.

[17] And the one woman said, O my lord, I and this woman dwell in one house; and I was delivered of a child with her in the house.

[18] And it came to pass the third day after that I was delivered, that this woman was delivered also: and we were together; there was no stranger with us in the house, save we two in the house.

[19] And this woman's child died in the night; because she overlaid it.

[20] And she arose at midnight, and took my son from beside me, while thine handmaid slept, and laid it in her bosom, and laid her dead child in my bosom.

[21] And when I rose in the morning to give my child suck, behold, it was dead: but when I had considered it in the morning, behold, it was not my son, which I did bear.

[22] And the other woman said, Nay; but the living is my son, and the dead is thy son. And this said, No; but the dead is thy son, and the living is my son. Thus they spake before the king.

It is hard to imagine how these two mothers must have looked to Solomon. They were prostitutes, outcasts from society. Normally they would not have been allowed in to see the king. Yet here they were, both claiming to be the mother of the living child.

Surely Solomon must have been reminded of what God had promised. If Solomon ever needed wisdom and an understanding heart, it was now. The only evidence he had to go on was the

word of these women. There were no other witnesses to the sup-
posed baby swap.

It is curious why the woman whose child died was eager to
have the living one. Having a child was evidence of her sinful
lifestyle. A dead child would be an easy way to hide her sin.
Whatever her reason, as the two mothers stood arguing before
the king, their maternal instincts came through clearly.

The King's Solution

Reading further in 1 Kings 3:24–28, we see how God granted
Solomon the wisdom to solve this problem.

> [24] And the king said, Bring me a sword. And they
> brought a sword before the king.
>
> [25] And the king said, Divide the living child in two,
> and give half to the one, and half to the other.
>
> [26] Then spake the woman whose the living child was
> unto the king, for her bowels yearned upon her son,
> and she said, O my lord, give her the living child, and
> in no wise slay it. But the other said, Let it be neither
> mine nor thine, but divide it.
>
> [27] Then the king answered and said, Give her the
> living child, and in no wise slay it: she is the mother
> thereof.
>
> [28] And all Israel heard of the judgment which the
> king had judged; and they feared the king: for they saw
> that the wisdom of God was in him, to do judgment.

King Solomon knew which woman was the real mother by
her own words; each mother gave away her own identity. The
fame of King Solomon's wisdom spread all over Israel. This short
story is used frequently as an example of Solomon's wisdom. It is
also one of the Bible's most stirring examples of a mother's love
put to the test.

We don't know what happened to the two women after
Solomon's decision; the Bible is silent. I can't help wonder why

God does not tell us more. Perhaps it is because the lesson to be learned is the faithfulness of God to Solomon in granting Him the wisdom He promised, rather than what happened to the women.

CLOSING THOUGHTS

Has God placed you in a position of leadership? Have you ever asked Him for wisdom? Maybe you are a mother of small children. Many times a day you need correct understanding to know what is right or wrong. If you have a teenager, as I do, you certainly need to ask God for wisdom!

In James 1:5–6a, God promises to give wisdom: *"If any of you lack wisdom, let him ask of God, that giveth to all men liberally, and upbraideth not; and it shall be given him. But let him ask in faith, nothing wavering."*

Why does the Bible say we need to ask for wisdom, believing we shall receive it? The answer is that true understanding comes from God and is visible in our lives only as we live in a way acceptable to Him. King Solomon wrote in Proverbs 9:10, *"The fear of the Lord is the beginning of wisdom."* "Fear" as used in this verse means reverence for God in our relationship with Him. The Bible tells us that we need to depend on God and put our trust in Him. This is what Solomon did. He talked with God— and gained great wisdom from God.

As Christian women, people who do not know the Lord as Savior may look to us for answers to their questions and problems. Like Solomon, if we seek God's wisdom, we can be witnesses to others that God can solve the problems of life.

If you do not have a personal faith in God, however, you cannot expect to have God's wisdom. To have that relationship, you must believe in the Lord Jesus Christ and accept His death on the Cross as payment for your sins. Ephesians 2:8–9 explains this: "For by grace are ye saved through faith; and that not of yourselves: it is the gift of God: Not of works, lest any man should boast."

After receiving the gift of salvation, you can look to God for the wisdom you need day by day. Also, you can ask for wisdom to help those who look to you for advice and help in their problems.

FOR DISCUSSION

1. What do you think was God's purpose for including this story in the Bible?
2. How did Solomon receive the wisdom he had?
3. Is it wrong to ask God for this kind of understanding in your life? Quote the Bible verse in which God promises to supply wisdom.
4. How far and to what lengths does a mother's love go?
5. Can you tell of a time when someone else's wisdom helped you? Can you tell of a time when you have been able to give wise advice to someone else?

CHAPTER 24

THE QUEEN OF SHEBA

SHE SEARCHED FOR WISDOM

The Queen and King Solomon

As women, we often desire something we don't have. In this study, we will see that the Queen of Sheba had all the world's material things she wanted, yet she longed for wisdom. She heard of King Solomon's wisdom. So the queen came to ask him questions and to hear his answers. 1 Kings 4:31 states that King Solomon was the wisest man on Earth. Because of that, he probably was extremely busy. In studying this true account, I was impressed that God took the time to answer the queen's questions.

When Solomon became king, God told him He would give him whatever he asked. Solomon requested wisdom, instead of wealth, fame, power, or anything else. God gave him wisdom plus the great wealth and honor he had not selfishly requested. This promise to Solomon is found in 1 Kings 3:10–12:

> [10] And the speech pleased the Lord, that Solomon had asked this thing.
>
> [11] And God said unto him, Because thou hast asked this thing, and hast not asked for thyself long life; neither hast asked riches for thyself, nor hast asked the life of thine enemies; but hast asked for thyself understanding to discern judgment;
>
> [12] Behold, I have done according to thy words: lo, I have given thee a wise and an understanding heart; so

that there was none like thee before thee, neither after
thee shall any arise like unto thee.

The Queen's Visit

The Lord did as He promised. He blessed Solomon in all
ways. The king's fame spread to the neighboring countries. The
Queen of Sheba heard about him, as we read in 1 Kings 10:1–3:

> ¹ And when the queen of Sheba heard of the fame
> of Solomon concerning the name of the LORD, she
> came to prove him with hard questions.
> ² And she came to Jerusalem with a very great train,
> with camels that bare spices, and very much gold, and
> precious stones: and when she was come to Solomon,
> she communed with him of all that was in her heart.
> ³ And Solomon told her all her questions: there was
> not any thing hid from the king, which he told her
> not.

She Fulfills Her Purpose

The Queen of Sheba came from the south to Jerusalem,
as the Bible clearly states, "to prove him with hard questions"
(1 Kings 10:1).

Her visit was unlike those of people from other nations who,
out of fear of Israel's strength, came to make peace with King
Solomon. The Queen of Sheba sought answers to the questions
deep in her heart. She hungered for truth.

The Bible completes the story by saying Solomon answered
all her questions. We don't know what her questions were, but
the important thing is that God made sure all of them were
answered.

She Acknowledges God

The queen looked at all of King Solomon's wealth. She
observed the way his servants ate. She considered the great size
of his kingdom. She looked at the temple Solomon had built for

God. We read her analysis in 1 Kings 10:6-9:

> ⁶ And she said to the king, It was a true report that I
> heard in mine own land of thy acts and of thy wisdom.
> ⁷ Howbeit I believed not the words, until I came, and
> mine eyes had seen it: and, behold, the half was not
> told me: thy wisdom and prosperity exceedeth the
> fame which I heard.
> ⁸ Happy are thy men, happy are these thy servants,
> which stand continually before thee, and that hear thy
> wisdom.
> ⁹ Blessed be the LORD thy God, which delighted
> in thee, to set thee on the throne of Israel: because the
> LORD loved Israel for ever, therefore made he thee
> king, to do judgment and justice.

Did you notice the Queen of Sheba gave credit to God? She acknowledged that Solomon's wisdom and wealth were blessings from God. We don't know if she became a follower of the true God, but she did acknowledge Him.

Acknowledgment Alone Isn't Enough

The queen knew God was the One who had blessed Israel. She even may have respected Him. This does not mean she personally accepted Him as her only God. Many people today are like the Queen of Sheba. Maybe you are like her. Don't be fooled, simply knowing that God exists does not mean you have a personal relationship with Him that will last for all of eternity. You must accept this personal relationship with Him through His Son, Jesus Christ. Acts 4:12 gives a clear explanation: *"Neither is there salvation in any other: for there is none other name under heaven given among men, whereby we must be saved."*

The Bible goes on to say that after the Queen of Sheba and Solomon exchanged gifts, she returned to her own country. We can only hope that the wisdom she sought after and the answers she found became a part of her life, and that she told what she had seen and heard to people in her own country.

Jesus Speaks of the Queen of Sheba

God's Word records nothing more about the Queen of Sheba's visit to Solomon until Jesus Christ lived on Earth 900 years later. During the ministry of Jesus, the religious leaders refused to accept that He was the Messiah. While Jesus was telling them how blind they were to the truth, He used the Queen of Sheba as an example. Jesus said in Matthew 12:42: *"The queen of the south shall rise up in the judgment with this generation, and shall condemn it: for she came from the uttermost parts of the earth to hear the wisdom of Solomon; and, behold, a greater than Solomon is here."*

Jesus makes the Queen of Sheba superior to the religious leaders because she traveled so far to hear Solomon. Jesus Christ, God in the flesh, was right there with them. He was greater than Solomon, yet they refused to hear His God-given truth. The Queen of Sheba sought wisdom, and God's Son holds her up as an example to those who refuse to hear and appreciate divine wisdom.

CLOSING THOUGHTS

The Queen of Sheba teaches us a valuable lesson. She hungered for wisdom. She went to the best source she knew and had her questions answered. The Bible does not tell us what she did with the answers once she got them, but we know she recognized the truth when she found it.

In the Sermon on the Mount, Jesus Christ said, *"Blessed are they which do hunger and thirst after righteousness: for they shall be filled"* (Matthew 5:6). If you desire to know the truth, God promises you will find it. But you need to seek real wisdom at its source. King Solomon said in Proverbs 9:10: *"The fear of the LORD is the beginning of wisdom."*

In order to make this truth of value in your life, you must personally accept Jesus Christ as your Savior. In John 14:6 Jesus says: *"I am the way, and the **truth**, and the life; no one comes unto the Father, but by me."*

Have you ever invited "the Truth" into your life? Why don't you do it right now? In the same way the Queen of Sheba poured out all her questions to Solomon, you can pour out all the questions in your heart to the One who is "greater than Solomon," Jesus Christ. I assure you that just as Solomon answered all the Queen's questions, Jesus Christ will meet all your needs.

FOR DISCUSSION

1. When did God give Solomon such great wisdom?
2. How did the Queen of Sheba's visit differ from those of other visitors to King Solomon?
3. How did Jesus use this story in his teachings?
4. Explain why the knowledge of truth is not the same thing as salvation from sin.
5. What valuable lesson can we learn from the Queen of Sheba?

CHAPTER 25

JEZEBEL

A WICKED QUEEN

Many of the women in the Bible loved God, and their lives show us lessons to apply to our Christian lives. That is not so, however, in the life of Jezebel. She was a woman whose life was filled with bad examples for us to avoid. She was a woman who hated God.

We like to admire and respect people. But sometimes it is helpful to have examples of what we should *not* be like. 2 Timothy 3:16 says, *"All scripture is given by inspiration of God, and is profitable for doctrine, for reproof, for correction, for instruction in righteousness."*

Jezebel's Background

In the Old Testament books of First and Second Kings, we find the story of Jezebel, a wicked queen. She was the daughter of a heathen king, who worshiped a false god named Baal, and wife to Ahab, king of Israel. At this time in history, Israel was divided in two. The northern kingdom was made up of 10 of the original 12 tribes of Israel and retained the name "Israel," while the two remaining tribes in the south became known as the nation of Judah.

The Bible does not tell us where or how Ahab and Jezebel met or under what circumstances they came to be married. But Ahab sinned against the commandments of God when he married a woman who worshiped false gods. 1 Kings 16:30–33 describes King Ahab:

³⁰ And Ahab the son of Omri did evil in the sight of the LORD above all that were before him.

³¹ And it came to pass, as if it had been a light thing for him to walk in the sins of Jeroboam the son of Nebat, that he took to wife Jezebel the daughter of Ethbaal king of the Zidonians, and went and served Baal, and worshipped him.

³² And he reared up an altar for Baal in the house of Baal, which he had built in Samaria.

³³ And Ahab made a grove; and Ahab did more to provoke the LORD God of Israel to anger than all the kings of Israel that were before him.

When Moses was leader of Israel, God gave these clear commandments: *"Thou shalt have no other gods before me. Thou shalt not make unto thee any graven image, or any likeness of any thing that is in heaven above, or that in the earth beneath, or that is in the water under the earth. Thou shalt not bow down thyself to them, nor serve them"* (Exodus 20:2–5).

Ahab sinned by marrying Jezebel, but even worse than that, he himself worshiped her gods and made idols. We read in 1 Kings 21:25: *"There was none like unto Ahab, which did sell himself to work wickedness in the sight of the Lord, whom Jezebel his wife stirred up."* What dreadful words for God to have to say about a man! Why would Ahab get involved in such wickedness? Looking at the character of his wife, Jezebel, gives us some clues.

Jezebel's Character

The Bible describes a series of events that show Jezebel as a strong-willed and forceful woman. She used her powers to destroy a king, to destroy her children, and to pollute an entire nation. She was a devout worshiper of the idol Baal, and supported Baal's priests. Her aim was to kill all the people who worshiped the Lord God of Israel.

Elijah's Challenge

History tells us that many cruel ceremonies accompanied the worship of Baal, including burning infants as a sacrifice. Into this idolatry and wickedness, God sent His prophet Elijah to confront King Ahab. Elijah fearlessly and publicly challenged the priests of Baal to a supreme test of power on Mount Carmel. The Lord worked a great miracle, and all the people knew that God was greater than Baal. After seeing God's power, the people *"fell on their faces and said, 'The Lord, He is God; the Lord, He is God'"* (1 Kings 18:39).

Jezebel's Response

Following the contest on Mount Carmel, the followers of God killed all the prophets of Baal. Jezebel was furious, and knowing how important Baal and the priests were to his wife, Ahab was frightened. 1 Kings 19:1–2 tell us:

> ¹ And Ahab told Jezebel all that Elijah had done, and withal how he had slain all the prophets with the sword.
>
> ² Then Jezebel sent a messenger unto Elijah, saying, So let the gods do to me, and more also, if I make not thy life as the life of one of them by to morrow about this time.

Ahab was the king, but Jezebel was a domineering wife who really ruled the kingdom. Everyone—including Elijah—feared her. She threatened Elijah with these words: *"So let the gods do to me, and more also, if I don't make thy life as one of them by tomorrow"* (1 Kings 19:2). God protected His prophet Elijah and provided him with food and rest.

Jezebel's Influence on Her Children

The Bible uses stories such as this to teach us how our life principles and convictions are passed on to our children and our grandchildren. The commandments that God gave to Moses in Exodus 20 are repeated in Deuteronomy 5:7–10:

> ⁷ Thou shalt have none other gods before me.
> ⁸ Thou shalt not make unto thee any graven image, or any likeness of any thing that is in heaven above, or that is in the earth beneath, or that is in the water under the earth:
> ⁹ Thou shalt not bow down thyself to them, nor serve them: for I the LORD thy God am a jealous God, visiting the iniquity of the fathers upon the children unto the third and fourth generation of them that hate me;

A heritage is the influence passed on from parent to child—whether for good or for evil. Can you imagine the kind of motherly influence Jezebel had? Jesus used a tree as an illustration of the continuing influence our lives have on other people. Matthew 7:16-18 says: *"Ye shall know them by their fruits. Do men gather grapes of thorns, or figs of thistles? Even so every good tree bringeth forth good fruit; but a corrupt tree bringeth forth evil fruit. A good tree cannot bring forth evil fruit, neither can a corrupt tree bring forth good fruit."*

We see the truth of this illustration in Jezebel's family. Her own father was a murderer. Her eldest son was a devout worshiper of Baal. Her daughter was a murderer. Her second son was as corrupt as she was. Her family carried on the influence of wickedness to at least the third generation. Jezebel and her children were the fruit of a corrupt tree.

God's Judgment on Jezebel

The Bible tells how God judged Jezebel. King Ahab wanted a vineyard owned by a man named Naboth. The king tried to buy it, but it wasn't for sale because it was Naboth's inheritance from his father. Ahab was depressed because Naboth refused to sell; he even stopped eating. When Jezebel heard about the situation, she promised to get the vineyard for Ahab. To do so, she planned and carried out Naboth's murder.

Once again, God sent Elijah to confront Ahab. Elijah pro-
nounced God's judgment on the king and his family for their
wickedness. The judgment was death. Everything happened
exactly the way Elijah said it would. Ahab was killed in his char-
iot during a war between the Israelites and the Syrians. Jezebel
died when she was thrown from a window and trampled under
the hooves of a horse. As Elijah had prophesied, her body was
eaten by dogs before she could be buried.

CLOSING THOUGHTS

Jezebel stands as proof that the wages of sin is death. God's
principle of reaping what you sow is vividly seen in the life of
Jezebel. If you sow good seed in your own life and in the lives of
children over whom you have influence, you—and they—will
reap God's blessing. The opposite of that is also true. If you sow
wickedness in your life and the lives of others, that evil legacy
will affect future generations. This is true in the lives of believers
in Jesus Christ as well as non-believers. Jesus died as the sacrifice
for our sin. When we receive Him as Savior, He forgives our sin,
but we often bear the consequences of our sin throughout our
lives.

Jezebel was the opposite of all God intends a woman to be.
Ahab was strongly influenced by his wife, but her powerful influence was for evil, not good. How different this story could have
been if Jezebel had learned to prompt her husband and children
to love God and follow His commandments.

Women such as Jezebel live today, also. They defy God. They
hate and harm God's people. But we do not have to be afraid of
them. 2 Thessalonians 1:7–9 tells what will become of men and
women who mock God and reject the good news of His beloved
Son: *"And to you who are troubled rest with us, when the Lord Jesus
shall be revealed from heaven with his mighty angels, In flaming fire taking vengeance on them that know not God, and that obey not the gospel*

of our Lord Jesus Christ: Who shall be punished with everlasting destruction from the presence of the Lord, and from the glory of his power."

I am sure all of us agree we would like to be the women God wants us to be. Jezebel's life should make us think about our own commitment—first to the Lord Jesus Christ, and then to our families.

FOR DISCUSSION

1. What was Ahab's sin that started all the trouble?
2. List three of Jezebel's characteristics.
3. Why was Elijah afraid of Jezebel?
4. List three lessons we can learn from the life of Jezebel.
5. What will be the final end of those who—like Jezebel—defy God?

CHAPTER 26

THE WIDOW
FROM ZAREPHATH

A WOMAN GIVEN TO HOSPITALITY

This is the story of a woman who, because of her hospitality to God's prophet Elijah, turned her sorrow into joy.

In His Word, God sometimes clearly states the names and backgrounds of some people we read about, but of others—such as this woman—we are told nothing. However, her faith and actions are recorded because God knew we needed those lessons.

The Situation

God told His people that if they obeyed Him, He would bless them. If they failed to obey Him, He would withhold His blessing. One blessing to be withheld was rain for their crops.

During the reign of King Ahab and Queen Jezebel—Israel's most wicked king and queen—Israel's spiritual condition was terrible. Elijah, God's prophet, appeared before the king and announced there would be no rain until he spoke again. This meant famine would cover the land. Elijah ran and hid as God had commanded him.

God's Provision for Elijah

First, God miraculously provided for Elijah by sending him to a hidden brook. But eventually the brook dried up. Then God told the prophet to go to Zarephath, a foreign city on the

Mediterranean Sea, where a widow would take care of him. The story is found in 1 Kings 17:9–10. The Lord said to Elijah:

> [9] Arise, get thee to Zarephath, which belongeth to Zidon, and dwell there: behold, I have commanded a widow woman there to sustain thee.
>
> [10] So he arose and went to Zarephath. And when he came to the gate of the city, behold, the widow woman was there gathering of sticks: and he called to her, and said, Fetch me, I pray thee, a little water in a vessel, that I may drink.

God commanded the widow to help Elijah, even though she lived in a nation that worshiped idols. Whether or not she knew God personally we do not know, but she certainly knew about Him after Elijah stayed with her.

The Widow's Need

When Elijah met the widow, she was gathering sticks to cook a final meal for herself and her son. Put yourself in her place. How would you have reacted to a stranger coming to your house asking for food and water when it had not rained for months? How eager would you have been to be hospitable?

The woman knew she was not prepared to feed a guest. Yet, she did not turn Elijah away. We read her reaction in 1 Kings 17:11–16:

> [11] And as she was going to fetch it, he called to her, and said, Bring me, I pray thee, a morsel of bread in thine hand.
>
> [12] And she said, As the LORD thy God liveth, I have not a cake, but an handful of meal in a barrel, and a little oil in a cruse: and, behold, I am gathering two sticks, that I may go in and dress it for me and my son, that we may eat it, and die.
>
> [13] And Elijah said unto her, Fear not; go and do as

thou hast said: but make me thereof a little cake first, and bring it unto me, and after make for thee and for thy son.

¹⁴ For thus saith the LORD God of Israel, The barrel of meal shall not waste, neither shall the cruse of oil fail, until the day that the LORD sendeth rain upon the earth.

¹⁵ And she went and did according to the saying of Elijah: and she, and he, and her house, did eat many days.

¹⁶ And the barrel of meal wasted not, neither did the cruse of oil fail, according to the word of the LORD, which he spake by Elijah.

The Need Supplied

By faith, this woman "went and did what God said to her" through Elijah. God kept His promise to supply flour and oil. Can you imagine the difference it made to have God's prophet in her home? All the widow's worries about providing food for herself and her son were eliminated. As the days turned to months, I am sure the widow and her son learned much about God. They probably came to feel very secure with Elijah in their home.

The Crisis

Then one day, the widow's son became sick and died. The woman was once again plunged into despair. First, she had lost her husband. Then because of the famine, she was not able to provide food for her son. God had met that need through Elijah. Now her son was dead. In her sorrow, the angry widow blamed the prophet's presence in her home for the death of her son. Perhaps she had become aware of her own sin as the prophet spoke to them of God. She immediately associated death as judgment for sin (1 Kings 17:18).

Elijah didn't try to answer the woman's accusation. Instead, he spoke graciously to her, as we read in 1 Kings 17:19–24:

[19] And he said unto her, Give me thy son. And he took him out of her bosom, and carried him up into a loft, where he abode, and laid him upon his own bed.

[20] And he cried unto the LORD, and said, O LORD my God, hast thou also brought evil upon the widow with whom I sojourn, by slaying her son?

[21] And he stretched himself upon the child three times, and cried unto the LORD, and said, O LORD my God, I pray thee, let this child's soul come into him again.

[22] And the LORD heard the voice of Elijah; and the soul of the child came into him again, and he revived.

[23] And Elijah took the child, and brought him down out of the chamber into the house, and delivered him unto his mother: and Elijah said, See, thy son liveth.

[24] And the woman said to Elijah, Now by this I know that thou art a man of God, and that the word of the LORD in thy mouth is truth.

It must have been hard for a grieving mother to wait downstairs. Time probably seemed to pass very slowly. But she waited, and once again she saw a miracle. As the story ends, she knew her guest was truly sent to her by God.

The Woman's Example

As the time of the drought drew to a close, Elijah had to leave. He was to announce that soon there would be rain again. We don't read or hear any more about the widow of Zarephath or her son in the Old Testament. But one day, while Jesus was teaching in a synagogue in His hometown, He used the example of the widow's hospitality. Luke 4:24–26 quotes Jesus as saying: *"Verily I say unto you, No prophet is accepted in his own country. But I tell you of a truth, many widows were in Israel in the days of Elias, when the heaven was shut up three years and six months, when great famine was throughout all the land; But unto none of them was Elias sent, save unto Sarepta, a city of Sidon, unto a woman that was a widow."*

Using this illustration, Jesus taught that just as the Gentile widow was kind to God's prophet, so He was accepted in Gentile hearts and lives, while being rejected by His own people.

CLOSING THOUGHTS

Hospitality is an important ministry for women. The apostle Paul includes hospitality as part of the duty of the Church in Romans 12:13: "Distributing to the necessity of saints; given to hospitality."

Paul also lists hospitality as part of the lifestyle for someone who qualifies as a pastor (or bishop) of the Church. *"A bishop then must be blameless, the husband of one wife, vigilant, sober, of good behavior, given to hospitality, apt to teach"* (1 Timothy 3:2).

Hospitality—opening your home to others in Christian love—is a ministry women can offer other women, families can show to other families, or couples to couples. Giving hospitality is a wonderful way to show the love of Christ to acquaintances as well as to strangers. Hebrews 13:2 commands: *"Be not forgetful to entertain strangers: for thereby some have entertained angels unawares."*

Not only does giving hospitality benefit the woman who is showing hospitality, everyone in the home benefits. 1 Peter 4:9 states, *"Use hospitality one to another without grudging."*

Ask God to show you ways you can open your home and use it for His glory.

FOR DISCUSSION

1. Why did Elijah go to Zarephath?
2. List two ways the widow's faith was tested.
3. In what way did she benefit by showing hospitality?

4. What did Jesus say about her?
5. Name three ways you can follow the widow's example of hospitality.

CHAPTER 27

THE WIDOW WHOSE OIL MULTIPLIED

A WOMAN WHO PAID HER DEBTS

God's Care for Widows and Orphans

The Bible has a lot to say about widows. Whether named or not, widows are of special concern to God. Many verses in the Bible give strong warnings to anyone who would in any way wrong a widow.

When God gave His laws to the Israelites, He laid down specific rules concerning the welfare and safety of widows. Many were similar to the rules about orphans. For example, we read in Exodus 22:22–24:

> [22] Ye shall not afflict any widow, or fatherless child.
>
> [23] If thou afflict them in any wise, and they cry at all unto me, I will surely hear their cry;
>
> [24] And my wrath shall wax hot, and I will kill you with the sword; and your wives shall be widows, and your children fatherless.

In the New Testament, James 1:27 gives a summary as to the way we should treat both widows and orphans: *"Pure religion and undefiled before God and the Father is this, To visit the fatherless and widows in their affliction, and to keep himself unspotted from the world."*

The Destitute Widow of a Prophet

In this Bible study, we find the story of a woman whose husband had loved the Lord, but had not done well in providing for his family. After his death, his widow was left with many debts and had no money to pay them. Her story begins in 2 Kings 4:1–4:

> ¹ Now there cried a certain woman of the wives of the sons of the prophets unto Elisha, saying, Thy servant my husband is dead; and thou knowest that thy servant did fear the LORD: and the creditor is come to take unto him my two sons to be bondmen.
>
> ² And Elisha said unto her, What shall I do for thee? tell me, what hast thou in the house? And she said, Thine handmaid hath not any thing in the house, save a pot of oil.
>
> ³ Then he said, Go, borrow thee vessels abroad of all thy neighbours, even empty vessels; borrow not a few.
>
> ⁴ And when thou art come in, thou shalt shut the door upon thee and upon thy sons, and shalt pour out into all those vessels, and thou shalt set aside that which is full.

The phrase "sons of the prophets" indicates the widow's husband had been a student of the prophet Elisha. Because of this, she felt free to ask Elisha for help. Not only was she in trouble because of her debts, but she had been threatened with the loss of her sons, who would be taken as slaves of the person to whom she was indebted.

Elisha was known for doing miracles through the power of God. This time, however, he simply asked the woman what she already had in her house. He then instructed her to act in faith with what was available.

We find a similar situation in the New Testament. We read in John chapter 6 that Jesus asked His disciples what was available to eat when it was time to feed five thousand men. The disciples answered: one boy's small lunch. Jesus took it and multiplied it, to meet the needs of the people.

Elisha told the widow to gather empty jars or pots from her neighbors. This woman's faith was outstanding. We read of no hesitation. She did exactly what she was told to do. What would have happened if she had not followed the instructions to get empty jars? She might have missed the miracle.

Miracles in Secret

Elisha told the woman to close her doors while she filled the jars. Perhaps one reason he said this was the disturbance it could have caused if everyone passing by had seen the oil multiplying. If she had filled the jars in plain view, it could easily have become a public display. Instead of God getting the credit, the people could have called the woman a miracle worker.

In the same way, several times during Jesus' earthly ministry, when someone asked for help, He told His disciples to close the doors, leaving the crowds outside. Then, in the privacy of the needy family, He performed His miracle.

In my own life, some of the greatest answers to prayer have come when God met a secret need. No one but God knew the need. When no one else knows, no one else can get the credit! Then the person receiving the answer to prayer must give the credit entirely to God.

Matthew 6:6 seems to teach this principle: *"But thou, when thou prayest, enter into thy closet, and when thou hast shut thy door, pray to thy Father which is in secret; and thy Father which seeth in secret shall reward thee openly."*

God Provided More Than "Enough"

We read the rest of the widow's story in 2 Kings 4:5–7:

> ⁵ So she went from him, and shut the door upon her and upon her sons, who brought the vessels to her; and she poured out.

⁶ And it came to pass, when the vessels were full, that she said unto her son, bring me yet a vessel. And he said unto her, There is not a vessel more. And the oil stayed.

⁷ Then she came and told the man of God. And he said, Go, sell the oil, and pay thy debt, and live thou and thy children of the rest.

Besides the woman's great faith, I find another lesson in this story. Even after all the jars were full, she did not assume the oil was for her. The woman did not rush ahead and make her own decision as to what God wanted her to do. Rather, she went back to Elisha and awaited further instructions. Following his words, she took the oil, sold it, and paid off all her debts to keep her sons free. In addition, she had enough money to live on.

Can you imagine the joy she had telling everyone, wherever she went, how God had met her needs? The widow had absolutely no doubt that it was God who had provided.

Not only did God provide enough for her immediate needs, but He also provided for the future. He gave more than she had asked for. This is similar to the story where Jesus fed the multitude with a little boy's lunch. In that account, twelve full baskets were left over.

CLOSING THOUGHTS

The apostle Paul expressed what this widow must have felt as she watched God work. He writes in Ephesians 3:20: *"Now unto him that is able to do exceeding abundantly above all that we ask or think, according to the power that worketh in us."*

The next time you find yourself in a place of need—regardless of what kind of need it is—this story will remind you how faithful God is to provide for you. Think about these verses.

"But my God shall supply all your need according to his riches in glory by Christ Jesus" (Philippians 4:19).

"And God is able to make all grace abound toward you; that ye, always having all sufficiency in all things, may abound to every good work" (2 Corinthians 9:8).

"If any of you lack wisdom, let him ask of God, that giveth to all men liberally, and upbraideth not; and it shall be given him" (James 1:5).

Today God still performs miracles meeting the needs of His children all around the world. Just as He did in this story, God often uses His servants as instruments in meeting the needs. It is wonderful to know He hears our prayers and, as the all-knowing and all-powerful God, is able to answer our prayers as He promises in Matthew 7:7–8: *"Ask, and it shall be given you; seek, and ye shall find; knock, and it shall be opened unto you; For every one that asketh receiveth; and he that seeketh findeth; and to him that knocketh it shall be opened."*

FOR DISCUSSION

1. In what circumstances did this woman find herself?
2. How did she show her complete obedience to Elisha?
3. How did God meet her need?
4. Who received the glory for this miracle?
5. Does God still meet needs today? How? Can you tell of a time when God met your needs?

CHAPTER 28

THE SHUNAMMITE WOMAN

A GENEROUS HOSTESS

We find another unnamed woman in this study. Since she was from the village of Shunem, she was known as the Shunammite.

The Bible describes her as a great or prominent woman. That probably means she was wealthy and influential in her community. In our study, however, we want to look at her spiritual insight, her generosity, her stability in crisis, and her obedience.

The Shunammite's Story

The story of the Shunammite woman is found in 2 Kings chapters 4 and 8. Her hospitality is shown in 2 Kings 4:8–11 by the way she opened her home to God's prophet Elisha:

8 And it fell on a day, that Elisha passed to Shunem, where was a great woman; and she constrained him to eat bread. And so it was, that as oft as he passed by, he turned in thither to eat bread.

9 And she said unto her husband, Behold now, I perceive that this is an holy man of God, which passeth by us continually.

10 Let us make a little chamber, I pray thee, on the wall; and let us set for him there a bed, and a table, and a stool, and a candlestick: and it shall be, when he

cometh to us, that he shall turn in thither.

¹¹ And it fell on a day, that he came thither, and he turned into the chamber, and lay there.

Her Spiritual Insight

We are not told whether this woman knew who Elisha was the first time she asked him to stop and eat at her house. But it does say that after several visits, she told her husband that she knew Elisha was a man of God.

Her Generosity

The woman realized Elisha needed a place for rest. She was perceptive to recognize how important it is to care for the physical and spiritual needs of others. She was also creative in the way she prepared a place for Elisha. I am sure her generosity meant much to Elisha each time he rested in that upper room.

As we continue with the story in 2 Kings 4:12–13, we see that Elisha tried to repay the Shunammite woman for her kindness:

¹² And he said to Gehazi his servant, Call this Shunammite. And when he had called her, she stood before him.

¹³ And he said unto him, Say now unto her, Behold, thou hast been careful for us with all this care; what is to be done for thee? wouldest thou be spoken for to the king, or to the captain of the host? And she answered, I dwell among mine own people.

From these verses, it is evident the woman shared her home out of sincere generosity and concern, wanting nothing in return. She was content without any honor or official recognition.

This is not the way we women usually think. Most often, we try to look good to other people. We want to make sure others see the good we do. Sometimes we do good works with wrong motives. We need to be reminded of what God's word says in 1 Samuel 16:7: *"The LORD seeth not as man seeth; for man looketh on the outward appearance, but the LORD looketh on the heart."*

One element was missing in the Shunammite woman's home, however. They had no children, and her husband was old (2 Kings 4:14). She didn't ask for a child when she was given a chance. Nevertheless, Elisha prophesied she would have a son, and the Bible tells us that, just as the prophet said, she conceived and bore a son.

Her Stability in Crisis

The next thing we read is a major crisis which hit just when everything was going along well and the family was happy. Isn't that the way things often happen? Continuing the story, we read in 2 Kings 4:18–21:

> [18] And when the child was grown, it fell on a day, that he went out to his father to the reapers.
>
> [19] And he said unto his father, My head, my head. And he said to a lad, Carry him to his mother.
>
> [20] And when he had taken him, and brought him to his mother, he sat on her knees till noon, and then died.
>
> [21] And she went up, and laid him on the bed of the man of God, and shut the door upon him, and went out.

The thing that stands out in this story is the Shunammite woman's silence even when faced with the death of her only son. There was no complaining or bitterness, no loud wailing; she simply set forth with determination to find the prophet Elisha. The section continues in 2 Kings 4:22–23:

> [22] She called her husband and said, Send me, I pray thee, one of the young men, and one of the asses, that I may run to the man of God, and come again.

²³ And he said, Wherefore wilt thou go to him today? It is neither new moon, nor Sabbath. And she said, It shall be well.

As the story goes on, the Shunammite woman journeyed with intensity of purpose to find the man of God. Before she arrived, Elisha saw her and recognized her from afar. He instructed his servant, *"Run now, I pray thee, to meet her, and say unto her, Is it well with thee? Is it well with thy husband? Is it well with thy child?"*

The woman answered, "It is well" (2 Kings 4:26). She knew her son was dead, so her simple words stating all was well showed her incredible faith in God's ability to help her.

When the woman found Elisha and told him what had happened, Elisha sent his servant ahead with instructions to lay his staff on the child's face. Later, when Elisha arrived with the woman, the servant informed him that the child had not awakened. 2 Kings 4:32–35 tells what happened as Elisha reached the upper room where the boy lay:

³² And when Elisha was come into the house, behold, the child was dead, and laid upon his bed.

³³ He went in therefore, and shut the door upon them twain, and prayed unto the LORD.

³⁴ And he went up, and lay upon the child, and put his mouth upon his mouth, and his eyes upon his eyes, and his hands upon his hands: and he stretched himself upon the child; and the flesh of the child waxed warm.

³⁵ Then he returned, and walked in the house to and fro; and went up, and stretched himself upon him: and the child sneezed seven times, and the child opened his eyes.

We are not told how long the child lived, but we assume he lived long enough to bring many more years of happiness to the home of the woman.

Her Obedience

We read of one other encounter between Elisha and this woman. Elisha told her that a seven-year famine would reach her land. He instructed her to take her son and go away until the famine was over. She immediately obeyed God's prophet, never taking time to think about all the wealth she was leaving behind.

At the end of the seven years, when the famine was over, she returned to her homeland to find others had claimed her possessions. Concerned for her son's inheritance, she went to the king to see if she could have her property returned to her. Elisha's servant was telling the king the story of her son being restored to life when she arrived. Because of her own testimony and that of Gehazi, the king restored all that she had owned (2 Kings 8:6).

From the beginning to the end of this woman's story, we see her faith, sincerity, stability in crisis, and endurance amid anxiety. She is an example of great faith. Even in dreadful circumstances, she did not doubt God's power and goodness.

CLOSING THOUGHTS

This woman received great rewards. First, she bore a son; then he was restored to her after his death; then all her possessions were returned to her. Most importantly, she was able to know God better by becoming the friend of His prophet Elisha.

As women of faith in God, if we live for Him as the Shunammite woman did, we can expect God to bless us, too. We may not receive the same kind of blessing, but we can be sure God looks with favor on those who obey His Word and provides for His servants. The kindness of God should draw us closer to Him day by day.

FOR DISCUSSION

1. Name three characteristics of this Shunammite woman.
2. When Elisha asked the Shunammite woman to leave her home, why did she choose to remain?

3. Describe two times this woman demonstrated great faith.
4. How did God reward her faith?
5. In what way can you show generosity to God's servants?

CHAPTER 29

THE SLAVE GIRL IN NAAMAN'S HOUSE

A WOMAN WHO REACTED QUICKLY

God knows how hard it is to forget what has happened in the past. In His Word, God gives several examples of women with difficult backgrounds, yet He used each one in a special way. Only a living, personal relationship with Jesus Christ can help us face the past. He removes guilt, heals pain, and makes us whole.

A Captive

Though this story is short, it is a clear example of how God can help us overcome our past. The story of this young girl and Naaman, the commander of the army of Aram, is found in 2 Kings 5:1–19.

Once again, the girl's name is not given. A slave would not be important enough to have her name recorded. It doesn't matter to God who we are in society; God sees our heart and knows our faith. Very little is written about this girl who served Naaman's wife, but we find part of her story in 2 Kings 5:2–3:

> ² And the Syrians had gone out by companies, and had brought away captive out of the land of Israel a little maid; and she waited on Naaman's wife.
>
> ³ And she said unto her mistress, Would God my lord were with the prophet that is in Samaria! for he would recover him of his leprosy.

A Foreigner

During an attack by enemy soldiers, this young girl was taken captive and carried away from her home country. The Bible does not give any indication as to where her family ended up after the enemy attack. She, however, was taken from all that was familiar and had to learn a whole new way of living. Surely this was not easy for her, and we can only imagine how homesick she must have been.

Putting ourselves in her place and thinking about what she had been through, how would we have reacted to our master's illness? Would we even have wanted to help him? She showed a genuine concern that only a life yielded to God could show. She spoke up with total confidence in God. It took a tremendous amount of courage to tell her mistress about the prophet who could help Naaman's leprosy. I wonder what she had seen or heard as a child that gave her such confidence in God and His prophet.

A Respected Person

How did this slave girl earn so much respect in Naaman's household that people would even listen to her? Why was this girl so sure Naaman could be healed? Where could she have gained so much spiritual insight at such a young age?

Perhaps more important questions are these: How would children of Christian families react today if they found themselves in hostile conditions? Do we train our children the way God has commanded us to? As a family, do we take time to remember what God has done for us? Would our children be able to state examples of what God has done to show His great power if they came under pressure like this slave girl?

The Bible doesn't give details as to what the girl said or what questions Naaman asked her. It does say that Naaman listened to her words. The rest of 2 Kings chapter 5 details Naaman's healing from leprosy. He went to the prophet Elisha, did what he was told to do, and was completely healed.

As if to confirm that this really happened, Jesus referred to this story in Luke 4:27: *"And many lepers were in Israel in the time of Elisha the prophet; and none of them was cleansed, saving Naaman the Syrian."*

CLOSING THOUGHTS

If this slave girl had chosen to be angry, to hold resentment and bitterness toward her captors, this true account would never have happened. Do you hold resentment for some bad experience in your childhood, teen years, or even adult life? If anyone had a right to blame God for what happened to her, this girl could have. But she did not.

Like her, we need to ask God to help us forget the things in our past that cause us trouble now. We need to keep accepting God's help for today. Then we can be women through whom God can work to show the world His love, power, and grace.

We need to accept God's will and the way He is working in our present life. The apostle Paul wrote in Philippians 3:13-14: *"Forgetting those things which are behind, and reaching forth to those things which are before, I press toward the mark of the prize of the high calling of God in Christ Jesus."*

Sometimes it helps to write out a list of the hurts, disappointments, and bitterness in your life. Read that list to your loving heavenly Father. Ask Him to cleanse your memory of those negative things and help you move ahead. 2 Corinthians 5:17 tells us: *"Therefore if any man be in Christ, he is a new creature: old things are passed away; behold all things are become new."*

FOR DISCUSSION

1. In what practical way did Naaman's young slave girl live her faith?
2. Name two things she could have become bitter about.
3. How did the girl influence her captor's life?

4. How should we, as Christian women, react when others
   wrong us?
5. What two qualities do you see in Naaman's slave girl that
   you would like to have in your own life?

CHAPTER 30

JEHOSHEBA

A WOMAN WHO SHOWED COURAGE
UNDER PRESSURE

All of us face pressure in our lives at some time or another. In this study, we will see the pressure Jehosheba faced in saving her nephew from murder.

Jehosheba's Background

The setting for this courageous act takes place in the land of Judah. The royal family we read about in this story was King Joram; his wife, Athaliah; and their children, Ahaziah and his sister, Jehosheba.

King Joram was 32 when he became king. His wife, Athaliah, was a daughter of wicked King Ahab. So it is not surprising that the Bible says Joram "did evil in the sight of the Lord." Joram died in great pain of an incurable disease. The people made Joram's youngest son, Ahaziah, king. We read these words about Ahaziah: *"He, too, walked in the ways of the house of Ahab, **for his mother encouraged him in doing wrong.**"* What terrible words to be said about any woman! Ahaziah was killed after ruling only one year. When the queen mother, Athaliah, heard about Ahaziah's death, she saw her chance to take control of the kingdom. She took the throne by killing all of Ahaziah's offspring—or so she thought—to make sure she would be the ruler.

Jehosheba's Courage

The story begins in 2 Kings 11:1–3:

> ¹ And when Athaliah the mother of Ahaziah saw that her son was dead, she arose and destroyed all the seed royal.
>
> ² But Jehosheba, the daughter of King Joram, sister of Ahaziah, took Joash the son of Ahaziah, and stole him from among the king's sons which were slain; and they hid him, even him and his nurse, in the bedchamber from Athaliah, so that he was not slain.
>
> ³ And he was with her hid in the house of the LORD six years. And Athaliah did reign over the land.

Jehosheba used a room in the house of the Lord to hide baby Joash (also spelled Jehoash). Since her husband, Jehoiada, was the high priest in charge of the temple, Joash was safe there. Besides, Athaliah worshiped the idol Baal and probably never entered the temple of the Lord. For six years, Jehosheba and her husband carefully nourished and taught Joash about the Lord.

Not only did it take courage to rescue the baby; it also took courage to teach Joash secretly while Athaliah ruled. The first lesson we learn from Jehosheba is to be courageous and persistent in doing what is right. It is easier to show courage for a short time, especially in a crisis, than it is to continue to do so day after day. It takes the grace of God in our lives to be consistently courageous, particularly if we are risking the lives of our loved ones. Yet the Bible says the Lord will reward those who persist in the face of difficulty. Galatians 6:9–10 gives the command: *"Let us not be weary in well doing: for in due season we shall reap, if we faint not. As we have therefore opportunity, let us do good unto all men, especially unto them who are of the household of faith."*

Jehosheba's Humility

The second lesson we learn from Jehosheba is steadfast humility. Her father had been king. She had just as much right to the throne as Athaliah, the king's second wife. Jehosheba could have been jealous. She could have made life miserable for her stepmother. Instead, she faithfully fulfilled her duty of teaching her nephew about the Lord to prepare him to be king.

The Presentation of Joash as Rightful King

During the seventh year of Joash's life, his uncle, the high priest, gathered together hundreds of mighty men and gave them specific instructions on how they were to guard the temple. When all was in order, he brought out Joash, presented him as the king's own son, and rightfully declared him the new king. This is what happened as we read in 2 Kings 11:12–16:

> [12] And he brought forth the king's son, and put the crown upon him, and gave him the testimony; and they made him king, and anointed him; and they clapped their hands, and said, God save the king.
>
> [13] And when Athaliah heard the noise of the guard and of the people, she came to the people into the temple of the LORD.
>
> [14] And when she looked, behold, the king stood by a pillar, as the manner was, and the princes and the trumpeters by the king, and all the people of the land rejoiced, and blew with trumpets: and Athaliah rent her clothes, and cried, Treason, Treason.
>
> [15] But Jehoiada the priest commanded the captains of the hundreds, the officers of the host, and said unto them, Have her forth without the ranges: and him that followeth her kill with the sword. For the priest had said, Let her not be slain in the house of the LORD.
>
> [16] And they laid hands on her; and she went by the way by the which the horses came into the king's house: and there was she slain.

In the same passage, we read that as soon as Joash became king, he destroyed the altars made for false gods, and the people once again served the living God. The Lord had not forgotten His people. He used the bravery of one woman to help fulfill His plan.

Jehosheba's husband carefully taught Joash when he was a small child, but the teaching didn't stop there. The high priest continued teaching the boy even after Joash became king. 2 Kings 12:2 says: *"And Jehoash did that which was right in the sight of the LORD all his days wherein Jehoiada the priest instructed him."*

CLOSING THOUGHTS

Diamonds are formed when carbon in the Earth is subjected to massive amounts of heat and pressure for many years. God often applies pressure to make human diamonds that show forth His beauty in their lives.

It is never easy to face pressure. We need to ask God to help us react with courage and boldness as Jehosheba did. She was not power hungry or reckless; rather, she was responsible and thoughtful. We can accomplish great things for God in spite of pressure, and in so doing, we become some of God's rare gems.

If you feel as if you are under heavy pressure in your life and have run out of courage, perhaps these words of David in Psalm 27:1, 3, 5 will give you the strength you need to keep on doing what is right: *"The LORD is my light and my salvation; whom shall I fear? the LORD is the strength of my life; of whom shall I be afraid? . . . Though an host should encamp against me, my heart shall not fear: though war should rise against me, in this will I be confident . . . For in the time of trouble he shall hide me in his pavilion: in the secret of his tabernacle shall he hide me; he shall set me up upon a rock."*

FOR DISCUSSION

1. What two great characteristics did Jehosheba show in her life?
2. For how long did she continue to show these characteristics?
3. How is God's justice seen in this story?
4. What spiritual principle found in Galatians 6:9 did Jeshosheba live out?
5. Describe a time in your life when good came out of what appeared to be a difficult situation.

CHAPTER 31

HULDAH

A WOMAN WHO SPOKE THE TRUTH

We women express ourselves in many ways. Our lifestyles, clothes, and actions all say something about who we are to those around us. We express ourselves most often with words, but silence can also be a way of letting others know our feelings.

The women in the Bible who had the biggest influence on those around them were women who lived close to God, respected His Word, and spoke with His authority. They earned the right to be heard because of their spiritual character.

Huldah's Background

Huldah was such a woman. Along with Deborah and Miriam, she was among the few women in the Old Testament who were given a place of authority. She was the wife of the keeper of the royal wardrobe and lived in Jerusalem during the reign of King Josiah.

King Josiah began his rule over the kingdom of Judah when he was only eight years old. His grandfather and his father had been wicked kings. But right from the beginning of his reign, Josiah was different. Our study of Huldah begins in 2 Kings 22:1–2:

> ¹ Josiah was eight years old when he began to reign, and he reigned thirty and one years in Jerusalem. And his mother's name was Jedidah, the daughter of Adaiah of Boscath.

² And he did that which was right in the sight of the
LORD, and walked in all the way of David his father,
and turned not aside to the right hand or to the left.

Notice that David is called "the father of Josiah." That is
because of the way the Hebrews thought of father-son relationships. Hundreds of years and several generations could pass
between two men in a direct ancestral line, and the former would
still be called the father of the latter. For example, Matthew 1:1
says that Jesus Christ is the son of David and the son of Abraham.
But David lived 1,000 years before Jesus, and Abraham lived
2,000 years before Him. In the same way, Josiah was the son of
David because he was in the royal line.

Josiah's Reign

When he had reigned for 18 years, King Josiah instructed a
scribe and other men to go to the temple, the house of the Lord.
The men were to ask the high priest, Hilkiah, how much money
was available, then give it to carpenters, builders, and masons to
buy supplies and repair the temple. While this was going on,
Hilkiah told Shaphan the scribe, "I have found the book of the
law in the house of the Lord." This, of course, was the Book of
the Law given to Moses many years before. The scribe, Shaphan,
read the book himself, then took it to the king and read the book
to him. We find King Josiah's reaction in 2 Kings 22:11–13:

¹¹ And it came to pass, when the king had heard the
words of the book of the law, that he rent his clothes.
¹² And the king commanded Hilkiah the priest, and
Ahikam the son of Shaphan, and Achbor the son of
Michaiah, and Shaphan the scribe, and Asahiah a
servant of the king's, saying,
¹³ Go ye, enquire of the LORD for me, and for the
people, and for all Judah, concerning the words of this
book that is found: for great is the wrath of the LORD
that is kindled against us, because our fathers have not

hearkened unto the words of this book, to do according unto all that which is written concerning us.

King Josiah immediately recognized the seriousness of the sinful condition of the people in the land. He was still young, only 26 years old, but he was a wise ruler.

Godly Counsel Given

The king knew he didn't have all the answers, so he sent for advice. Two well-known prophets of God, Jeremiah and Zephaniah, lived during this time. But the high priest and other men did not go to those prophets to ask counsel. Instead, they went to a prophetess named Huldah. We pick up the story again in 2 Kings 22:14-17:

> ¹⁴ So Hilkiah the priest, and Ahikam, and Achbor, and Shaphan, and Asahiah, went unto Huldah the prophetess, the wife of Shallum the son of Tikvah, the son of Harhas, keeper of the wardrobe; (now she dwelt in Jerusalem in the college;) and they communed with her.
>
> ¹⁵ And she said unto them, Thus saith the LORD God of Israel, Tell the man that sent you to me,
>
> ¹⁶ Thus saith the LORD, Behold, I will bring evil upon this place, and upon the inhabitants thereof, even all the words of the book which the king of Judah hath read:
>
> ¹⁷ Because they have forsaken me, and have burned incense unto other gods, that they might provoke me to anger with all the works of their hands; therefore my wrath shall be kindled against this place, and shall not be quenched.

Since the nation of Israel was already living sinfully when Josiah became king, it took courage for Huldah to give such a strong warning. As we read other verses in God's Word, we find that many prophets and others who spoke out for God were hated and sometimes even killed. For example, when Elijah predicted a drought, King Ahab was so angry that Elijah had to hide to save his life. In this account, we find that Huldah, because of her love and devotion to God, spoke the truth without fear. She told the men to tell the king what God said. She was careful to say, "Thus saith the Lord."

Reading 2 Kings 22:18–20, we see that King Josiah recognized the need to correct the evil ways of his nation. Because of Josiah's reaction, Huldah told the king of the Lord's compassion and forgiveness:

[18] But to the king of Judah which sent you to enquire of the LORD, thus shall ye say to him, Thus saith the LORD God of Israel, As touching the words which thou hast heard;

[19] Because thine heart was tender, and thou hast humbled thyself before the LORD, when thou heardest what I spake against this place, and against the inhabitants thereof, that they should become a desolation and a curse, and hast rent thy clothes, and wept before me; I also have heard thee, saith the LORD.

[20] Behold therefore, I will gather thee unto thy fathers, and thou shalt be gathered into thy grave in peace; and thine eyes shall not see all the evil which I will bring upon this place. And they brought the king word again.

The high priest and the other men took Huldah's message back to the king. This shows their own respect for her. They might have said, "Maybe the king won't like what she said would happen; let's find someone else to give him the bad news." Or they might have tried to find a more favorable prophecy from another source.

Josiah's Reaction

When King Josiah heard the message God spoke through Huldah, he gathered all the people—from the least to the greatest—together in the Lord's house. He read all the words of the Book of the Law to the congregation. Then, setting the example, Josiah made a public commitment to obey God. The people joined with him in a solemn covenant before God, to follow the Lord and keep His commands and decrees with their whole heart and soul.

At a time of crisis in the kingdom of Judah, it was a woman, Huldah, who was walking so closely to God that she was ready to speak for Him. She had the courage to do so with honesty. Because of Huldah, the king learned what he and his nation needed to do in order to keep them from the judgment and punishment they deserved.

CLOSING THOUGHTS

Huldah's confidence was in the Lord God. God still uses women today to speak out without fear, and with confidence in Him. King Josiah's forefather David knew the courage gained from such confidence in the Lord. He wrote these verses in Psalm 27:1 and 27:14: *"The LORD is my light and my salvation; whom shall I fear? the LORD is the strength of my life; of whom shall I be afraid? . . . Wait on the LORD: be of good courage, and he shall strengthen thine heart: wait, I say, on the LORD."*

Ask God to help you live with confidence in Him, and speak out for truth and righteousness.

FOR DISCUSSION

1. Describe Huldah's background and the times in which she lived.
2. What kind of king was Josiah?
3. Why did he respect the counsel of Huldah?
4. In what way did Huldah demonstrate courage?
5. How was Huldah an example of good leadership?

CHAPTER 32

ESTHER

A BEAUTIFUL, COURAGEOUS QUEEN: PART I

God has included the lives of women in His Word so we may learn from them. We women must never think we are not important, or that God uses and works only through men. The woman we will study in this two-part lesson is a good example. We will look at the life of Queen Esther, for whom the Old Testament book is named. Only one other book, Ruth, bears the name of the woman around whom the narrative centers.

Esther's Background

Esther's name means "star." That is a good description of her life, for she was a shining light for her people. Esther was a Jewess who, along with her family, was carried into captivity about 600 years before Christ's birth.

Her father was Abihail, who lived in Shushan, the royal city of Persia. After her parents died, Esther's cousin Mordecai, a palace official, became her guardian. Esther was obedient to him. Even after she became queen, she followed Mordecai's advice.

The Book of Esther

The book of Esther has an outstanding feature among the books of the Bible. Along with Song of Solomon, it shares the distinction of not once mentioning the word "God." Yet as you read the fast-moving story, you see God in control, perfectly fulfilling His divine will and purpose.

Esther's name appears 55 times in the book that bears her name. No other woman's name is mentioned that many times in the Bible.

The book of Esther is still read in Jewish synagogues around the world each year in the middle of March during the Feast of Purim. In our study of Esther, we will see why this feast is so important to the Jewish people.

Esther Chosen as Queen

We assume Esther lived quietly with her cousin Mordecai. At this time, Xerxes was the king of Persia. (His Hebrew name was Ahasuerus.) He ruled over 127 provinces from present-day India to Ethiopia.

King Xerxes gave an elaborate party for his nobles and officials. For 180 days, the king displayed the wealth of his vast empire. Then he gave a banquet for his military leaders, princes, and nobles lasting another seven days. Queen Vashti also gave a banquet for the noblewomen. On the seventh day, when the king and the men were in high spirits from the food and wine, King Xerxes commanded Queen Vashti to appear before the men. He wanted her to wear her royal crown and display her beauty before them. This was totally against the custom of Persian women. They were usually kept hidden away from the eyes of unknown men.

The queen refused to appear before the men at this drunken party. King Xerxes became furious and burned with anger. The king asked his law experts what he should do. They convinced the king that Queen Vashti's conduct would become known to all the women in his empire, and all women would disobey their husbands, causing disrespect and discord. The advisors suggested that King Xerxes write a law saying Vashti was never again to come into his presence and that a search would be made for a new queen. Esther 2:2–4, 8–9 gives the account:

² Then said the king's servants that ministered unto him, Let there be fair young virgins sought for the king:

³ And let the king appoint officers in all the provinces of his kingdom, that they may gather together all the fair young virgins unto Shushan the palace, to the house of the women, unto the custody of Hege the king's chamberlain, keeper of the women; and let their things for purification be given them:

⁴ And let the maiden which pleaseth the king be queen instead of Vashti. And the thing pleased the king; and he did so.

⁸ So it came to pass, when the king's commandment and his decree was heard, and when many maidens were gathered together unto Shushan the palace, to the custody of Hegai, that Esther was brought also unto the king's house, to the custody of Hegai, keeper of the women.

⁹ And the maiden pleased him, and she obtained kindness of him; and he speedily gave her things for purification, with such things as belonged to her, and seven maidens, which were meet to be given her, out of the king's house: and he preferred her and her maids unto the best place of the house of the women.

It appears that Esther found favor in the eyes of the king's representative even before she appeared before the king. She was given the best of everything, and kept in special lodgings. Finally the day came when it was Esther's turn to go before the king. The Bible continues in Esther 2:15–17:

¹⁵ Now when the turn of Esther, the daughter of Abihail the uncle of Mordecai, who had taken her for his daughter, was come to go in unto the king, she required nothing but what Hegai the king's chamber-

lain, the keeper of the women, appointed. And Esther obtained favour in the sight of all them that looked upon her.

¹⁶ So Esther was taken unto king Ahasuerus into his house royal in the tenth month, which is the month Tebeth, in the seventh year of his reign.

¹⁷ And the king loved Esther above all the women, and she obtained grace and favour in his sight more than all the virgins; so that he set the royal crown upon her head, and made her queen instead of Vashti.

Esther must have been a beautiful young woman. Yet even though she would be queen of one of the most powerful empires of the world, she did not become proud. She learned how to manage her power wisely. Esther's wisdom grew as she followed the advice of her cousin. This is clearly seen in Esther 2:20: *"Esther had not yet shewed her kindred nor her people; as Mordecai had charged her: for Esther did the commandment of Mordecai, like as when she was brought up with him."*

Why was it so important that Esther not show her true identity? By choosing Esther as his queen, King Xerxes was acting contrary to Persian law. The law said the king must marry a woman from one of the seven great Persian families in order to preserve the royal line. God, as He guided in perfect control, used Mordecai to help Esther keep her identity a secret until it was God's time to make it known.

CLOSING THOUGHTS

We can learn from Esther even at this early point in her story. We see that she was a woman who obeyed her guardian. We, too, need to respectfully obey those whom God has set over us, such as our parents and others in authority when we are young, and those to whom we pledge our allegiance, such as our husbands.

It is important to teach children to obey rightful authority. If Esther had not learned to obey her parents, it would have been harder for her to submit to Mordecai's authority. We do children a big favor in teaching them the importance of obedience. The Bible says in Ephesians 6:1–2: *"Children, obey your parents in the Lord: for this is right. Honour thy father and mother; which is the first commandment with promise."*

FOR DISCUSSION

1. What is unusual about the book of Esther?
2. Describe Esther's background?
3. Under what circumstances did Esther become the queen?
4. Why could Esther not reveal her nationality?
5. Why is it important to teach children to obey authority?

CHAPTER 33

ESTHER

A BEAUTIFUL, COURAGEOUS QUEEN: PART 2

In our previous study of Esther, we learned about her background and how she was chosen as queen. We also saw her obedience to her cousin Mordecai.

As we continue with Esther's story, we will see how she risked her life to save the lives of her people, the Jews. Esther showed wisdom, self-control, and the ability to put others ahead of herself—all lessons and examples we need to follow.

Esther Learns About Wicked Haman's Plot

According to Esther chapter 4, the queen received a report from her servants that Mordecai was dressed in sackcloth and ashes, a sign of great mourning. Esther sent servants to ask Mordecai what was wrong. Esther soon learned a man named Haman was plotting the destruction of the Jews. The king had elevated Haman to a place of honor above his other officials. All the king's officials knelt down and paid homage to Haman, but Mordecai would not do so. As a Jew, Mordecai believed only God should be given honor in that way. So Haman hated Mordecai. Since Haman had favor with the king, he convinced the king to make a decree to destroy the Jews. The king, however, did not know his own wife was Jewish!

Mordecai's Advice to Esther

Mordecai's instruction to Esther was that she should make an appeal for her people directly to the king. Esther told her cousin she could not do that because the law said any man or woman who approached the king without being summoned would be put to death. We read Mordecai's response in Esther 4:13–17:

¹³ Then Mordecai commanded to answer Esther, Think not with thyself that thou shalt escape in the king's house, more than all the Jews.

¹⁴ For if thou altogether holdest thy peace at this time, then shall there enlargement and deliverance arise to the Jews from another place; but thou and thy father's house shall be destroyed: and who knoweth whether thou art come to the kingdom for such a time as this?

¹⁵ Then Esther bade them return Mordecai this answer,

¹⁶ Go, gather together all the Jews that are present in Shushan, and fast ye for me, and neither eat nor drink three days, night or day: I also and my maidens will fast likewise; and so will I go in unto the king, which is not according to the law: and if I perish, I perish.

¹⁷ So Mordecai went his way, and did according to all that Esther had commanded him.

Notice how much Esther and Mordecai loved and respected each other. They worked together. Esther courageously and unselfishly agreed to the challenge her cousin gave her. But realizing the danger and importance of what she had agreed to do, she asked all the Jews to pray and fast with her. Esther teaches us three important lessons in this section:

- When we are faced with difficult circumstances, it is usually best to follow wise guidance such as Esther received from Mordecai.
- Esther saw the value in securing the cooperation of fellow believers in prayer and fasting before starting her difficult assignment.

- Esther shows us that we should use our God-given position and influence to help God's people, rather than trying to protect our own selfish interests.

Esther was willing to deny herself for the good of her people. Her life is a great example of how God can work through women.

Esther Puts Her Life in Jeopardy

After the fasting and praying, Esther prepared herself and went to the king. Esther 5:2–5 tells what happened:

> ² And it was so, when the king saw Esther the queen standing in the court, that she obtained favour in his sight: and the king held out to Esther the golden sceptre that was in his hand. So Esther drew near, and touched the top of the sceptre.
> ³ Then said the king unto her, What wilt thou, queen Esther? and what is thy request? it shall be even given thee to the half of the kingdom.
> ⁴ And Esther answered, If it seem good unto the king, let the king and Haman come this day unto the banquet that I have prepared for him.
> ⁵ Then the king said, Cause Haman to make haste, that he may do as Esther hath said. So the king and Haman came to the banquet that Esther had prepared.

When the king and Haman came to her banquet, Esther requested that they come to a second dinner. The Lord obviously guided her hesitation. One sleepless night between the two banquets, the king had his servants read to him from his record books. He learned that Mordecai had saved him from possible assassination and had never been rewarded for his loyalty.

This explains why the first banquet was not the right time for Esther to tell the king about Haman's plot. Most people, but especially women, find it hard to wait for God's timing. We want everything to happen right away. But waiting is important to our growth as Christians. God is sovereign and in perfect control of time. We would eliminate much worry if we could only grasp this truth.

Esther Reveals Haman's Wickedness

As we conclude the story, we read in Esther 7:2–6, 10 what happened at the second banquet Esther held for the king and Haman.

> ² And the king said again unto Esther on the second day at the banquet of wine, What is thy petition, queen Esther? and it shall be granted thee: and what is thy request? and it shall be performed, even to the half of the kingdom.
>
> ³ Then Esther the queen answered and said, If I have found favour in thy sight, O king, and if it please the king, let my life be given me at my petition, and my people at my request:
>
> ⁴ For we are sold, I and my people, to be destroyed, to be slain, and to perish. But if we had been sold for bondmen and bondwomen, I had held my tongue, although the enemy could not countervail the king's damage.
>
> ⁵ Then the king Ahasuerus answered and said unto Esther the queen, Who is he, and where is he, that durst presume in his heart to do so?
>
> ⁶ And Esther said, The adversary and enemy is this wicked Haman. Then Haman was afraid before the king and the queen.
>
> ¹⁰ So they hanged Haman on the gallows that he had prepared for Mordecai. Then was the king's wrath pacified.

We see how Esther saved the lives of all the Jewish people, including her own. When Jews across the empire heard how

Esther had saved their lives, they rejoiced. They still celebrate this deliverance in a special event called the Feast of Purim.

After Haman was killed, Queen Esther and Mordecai won even greater respect from the king and were rewarded with greater authority. The Lord used Esther's testimony to the king about the plot against the Jews to save them. At the beginning, Esther did not know whether or not the king would receive her, but she went to him because that was the right thing to do. It is likewise important for us to be faithful in our witness. We do not know how or when someone may respond to our testimony for the Lord.

CLOSING THOUGHTS

Esther was true to her family and her people. In an hour of crisis, she was not ashamed of her race and did not forget her own people. Some women try to hide or forget their roots, especially if there is something negative in their backgrounds they would not want anyone to know about. Sad to say, when God blesses some women with wealth and possessions, they forget their families and the place they were raised. Some go so far as to refuse to acknowledge their parents or be reminded of their poor background.

Esther was not like that. She risked her own life in order to save the lives of the Jewish people. Each of us as Christian women should remember our own families, as well as our brothers and sisters in God's family. If, like Esther, we are willing to let God use us wherever He puts us, the Church would be much stronger and happier.

Esther's testimony to the Persian king showed love for her people. Likewise, the way we treat God's people is a witness of our faith. We need to ask the Lord to help us know how to show His love in whatever circumstance we find ourselves. Paul wrote in Galatians 6:2: *"Bear ye one another's burdens, and so fulfil the law of Christ."*

We can best summarize Esther's life as one of service with bravery in the face of fear, of intelligence, deep insight and prudence. The question we need to answer is, "Could this be said of me?"

FOR DISCUSSION

1. When Esther realized her life was in danger, how did she respond?
2. What three lessons can we learn from Esther's life?
3. In what ways can we see God's blessing in Esther's life?
4. Why is it so hard to wait for God's timing?
5. Why do the Jews continue to celebrate the Feast of Purim?

CHAPTER 34

JOB'S WIFE

A WOMAN WHO WATCHED
HER HUSBAND SUFFER

The trial of Job is the subject of one of the earliest written books in the Bible. Job went through severe testing. Part of his suffering was physical, and part was emotional and mental. Through it all, Job did not deny his faith in God. His faith has been an example to Christians everywhere to this very day.

Background of the Story

In the first chapter of Job, we read that he was a wealthy man who feared God and walked uprightly. He and his wife had seven sons and three daughters. Job faithfully made sacrifices to God on behalf of his family. He said, "Perhaps my children have sinned and cursed God in their hearts." From a human perspective, no one could find fault with Job.

In Job 1:6–12, we read a fascinating conversation. Satan told God the only reason Job was so righteous and faithful was because God had blessed him so much. If all his blessings were taken away, Job would curse God, Satan reasoned.

God, in His perfect wisdom and knowledge, told Satan he could do anything to Job except take his life. God had at least two purposes in permitting Satan to test Job:

- to prove that Satan was wrong about Job's character and reason for serving God, and
- to use the trial to draw Job closer to Himself.

Our story begins in Job 1:13–19, 22. Keep in mind that whatever happened to Job had an effect on his whole family, including his wife:

> [13] And there was a day when his sons and his daughters were eating and drinking wine in their eldest brother's house:
>
> [14] And there came a messenger unto Job, and said, The oxen were plowing, and the asses feeding beside them:
>
> [15] And the Sabeans fell upon them, and took them away; yea, they have slain the servants with the edge of the sword; and I only am escaped alone to tell thee.
>
> [16] While he was yet speaking, there came also another, and said, The fire of God is fallen from heaven, and hath burned up the sheep, and the servants, and consumed them; and I only am escaped alone to tell thee.
>
> [17] While he was yet speaking, there came also another, and said, The Chaldeans made out three bands, and fell upon the camels, and have carried them away, yea, and slain the servants with the edge of the sword; and I only am escaped alone to tell thee.
>
> [18] While he was yet speaking, there came also another, and said, Thy sons and thy daughters were eating and drinking wine in their eldest brother's house:
>
> [19] And, behold, there came a great wind from the wilderness, and smote the four corners of the house, and it fell upon the young men, and they are dead; and I only am escaped alone to tell thee.
>
> [22] In all this Job sinned not, nor charged God foolishly.

Job's Wife

But what about Job's wife? As happens so often in Scripture, we do not know her name. Job's trials, and his reaction to them, are often discussed and preached about, but we almost never think about his wife. We know she, too, was deeply affected by what happened to her husband. She, too, lost everything. She was the wife of a rich man. She lived in abundance, wanting for nothing. Not only did she suddenly loose all her wealth; she also suffered the death of *all* her children. She had carried those ten children though childbirth and watched them grow. Now they were all dead!

If you know someone who has experienced the death of even one child, you know how difficult that can be. We can only imagine the depth of the sorrow Job's wife must have felt in the loss of all her children.

As if that were not enough, Satan continued to torment Job. His next attack afflicted Job's body with boils and tremendous pain. It is often easier to bear pain ourselves than to stand by helplessly and watch someone we love suffer.

At this point, when she saw how Job suffered, her faith in God broke down. In her grief, she cried out to her husband, "Are you still holding on to your integrity? Curse God and die" (Job 2:9).

If we had been in the place of Job's wife, I think many of us would have felt just as she did. Of course, that does not justify her reaction. She actually urged her husband to curse God! Perhaps she thought if he cursed God, he would be struck dead and his suffering would end.

Job's response to his wife is found in Job 2:10: *"Thou speakest as one of the foolish women speaketh. What? shall we receive good at the hand of God, and shall we not receive evil? In all this did not Job sin with his lips."*

The Bible does not say what her reaction was, but it could be that Job's faith helped his wife in her time of weakness. Notice carefully, even though her faith failed just when her husband needed her most, she stayed beside him. She did not leave him to suffer alone, nor did she divorce him. They remained husband and wife throughout the entire ordeal.

Job 19:17 gives Job's lament that even his breath is offensive to his wife. She must have stood close enough to him to notice this side effect of his ordeal; his diseased body made his breath foul. Likely she tried to comfort Job and help him whenever possible.

The Blessings of God Restored

The Bible completes the narrative for us. When Job's testing was finished, and God said it was enough, Job had remained true to God and successfully proved Satan's accusations were wrong.

God in His love restored Job's health and wealth. In Job 42: 12–15, we read that God returned to Job *and* his wife more material wealth than before. They also had seven more sons and three more daughters who were known as the most beautiful women in the land.

Though the book of Job doesn't mention his wife in the closing chapters, she must have been there to share in the joy of God's blessings once more in their home.

CLOSING THOUGHTS

The book of Job teaches us so much. Although the events mainly happened to Job, his wife was there the whole time. We see that abundant blessing often follows severe testing. Sometimes, when we are going through the trial, we don't understand. We get depressed and think God has forgotten us and will never bless us again. That is not true.

Sometimes a trial proves to be a blessing in disguise. God, who knows all aspects of our lives, sometimes uses testing to cleanse us of a flaw we thought no one could see. When the trial is over, our lives are more beautiful, our testimonies more powerful, or our prayers much deeper because of God's mercy in letting us be tested.

Job must have understood this concept, as he wrote these words in Job 23:10: *"But he knoweth the way that I take: when he hath tried me, I shall come forth as gold."*

Gold jewelry is highly regarded all over the world. Yet before it becomes beautiful in our eyes, it has to go through hot fires to remove all the impurities. Only then can it be made into the beautiful jewelry both men and women admire.

It is encouraging to know that God is in control and knows everything. Nothing can come into our lives without His knowledge and control. The Women's Devotional Bible (Zondervan © 1990, p. 318) gives this insight: "Job presents a striking example of the news behind the news—of God at work behind the scenes of human suffering. After numerous attempts by Job and his friends to uncover the reasons for his suffering, God Himself enters the dialogue with a majestic description of His power and love. God may not answer all your questions about life's suffering. But realize that God does control Satan, who can go no further than God allows."

In 1 Corinthians 10:13, we read this promise: *"There hath no temptation taken you but such as is common to man; but God is faithful, who will not suffer you to be tempted above that ye are able; but will with the temptation make a way of escape, that ye may be able to bear it."*

No matter what our circumstances may be, let us do as Job—and perhaps his wife with him—did: worship God and say, *"Blessed be the name of the Lord"* (Job 1:21).

FOR DISCUSSION

1. Why do you think God allowed Satan to bring suffering to Job, his wife, and his family?
2. Briefly describe the ways Job's wife suffered.
3. Why did Job's wife's faith weaken?
4. How is she an example to others in her marriage commitment?
5. Think of the trials *you* have had in your life. How did you react to them? Did you follow Job's example?

CHAPTER 35

MARY

MOTHER OF JESUS: PART 1

This is the first part in our study of Mary, the mother of Jesus. Throughout these lessons, we will discuss Mary's background, God's choice of her to be the mother of Jesus, her response to His choice, her submission, her service, and her sorrow. It is my prayer that together we will learn how we can live daily with the same godly spirit Mary had.

The name Mary is one of the most common names given to girls around the world. It takes many forms, such as Maria, Marie, or Miriam. One form of the name occurs in the Old Testament: Naomi changed her name to "Mara" to describe her sorrow and bitter affliction. Mary, the mother of Jesus, also knew great sorrow in her life.

Mary's Background

Apart from her cousin, Elizabeth, nothing is mentioned in the Bible concerning Mary's family. We know that she became the wife of Joseph, a man from Nazareth who was the son of Jacob. Scripture tells us that both Joseph and Mary came from the tribe of Judah and were descendants of David. This is told to us in Luke 2:3–5, where it explains how each person had to return to his own city to be taxed. Mary and Joseph both went to Bethlehem to pay their taxes. In Romans 1:3, Jesus is said to be of *"the seed of David according to the flesh."* His only connection with human flesh is through Mary, descended from David.

We read that throughout Jesus' earthly life, Nazareth is referred to as His hometown. Jesus lived in the home of a carpenter, undoubtedly a humble home in a lowly town. This is not where you would expect God's Son to be raised. In John 1:46, Nathaniel asks: *"Can any good thing come out of Nazareth?"*

God's Chosen Vessel

God's selection of Mary to be the mother of His own beloved Son is as hard for us to understand as the conception of Jesus by the Holy Spirit in her virgin womb. Mary, herself, was born in the same way as any other man or woman. She had a sinful nature. She had human limitations and faults. She needed a Savior just like every other person. She was no different physically than we are. Yet she was God's divine choice to give birth to Jesus Christ. She was the one chosen to nurse and care for Him through infancy, lovingly guide Him through boyhood, and with motherly wisdom prepare Him for manhood.

Mary's Character

Although it is true that Mary was a woman just like us, we need to recognize that she had qualities we would do well to cultivate in our lives. In Luke 1:26–31, we read of the angel Gabriel's visit to Mary when her cousin, Elizabeth, was six months pregnant:

> [26] And in the sixth month the angel Gabriel was sent from God unto a city of Galilee, named Nazareth,
>
> [27] To a virgin espoused to a man whose name was Joseph, of the house of David; and the virgin's name was Mary.
>
> [28] And the angel came in unto her, and said, Hail, thou that art highly favoured, the Lord is with thee: blessed art thou among women.
>
> [29] And when she saw him, she was troubled at his saying, and cast in her mind what manner of salutation this should be.

³⁰ And the angel said unto her, Fear not, Mary: for thou hast found favour with God.

³¹ And, behold, thou shalt conceive in thy womb, and bring forth a son, and shalt call his name JESUS.

The fact that Mary was a virgin is clearly stated in God's Word. This fact shows that she led a morally pure life.

Gabriel honors Mary by addressing her with the words "Hail favored one! The Lord is with you." Mary demonstrated *humility* because the Bible says she was troubled by these words of praise. She had no idea why she should be addressed in this way. The account continues in Luke 1:34–35 and 38:

³⁴ Then said Mary unto the angel, How shall this be, seeing I know not a man?

³⁵ And the angel answered and said unto her, The Holy Ghost shall come upon thee, and the power of the Highest shall overshadow thee: therefore also that holy thing which shall be born of thee shall be called the Son of God.

³⁸ And Mary said, Behold the handmaid of the Lord; be it unto me according to thy word. And the angel departed from her.

Not only did Mary demonstrate purity and humility; these verses show her *faith and trust* in God. Put yourself in Mary's place; imagine how the angel's words would affect your life. Mary asked Gabriel an intelligent question: how could she give birth to a son since she was a virgin?

Following the explanation of how this miracle would take place—even though she didn't understand it—Mary, by faith, willingly yielded her body for the Lord's use. She said: *"Behold, the handmaid of the Lord; be it unto me according to thy word"* (Luke 1:38).

By saying those words, Mary not only showed faith, but also *submission* to the will of God. We cannot understand how the

Holy Spirit fused together Deity and humanity in Mary's womb. But when He did, all of Scripture was accurately fulfilled in the virgin birth of Jesus Christ. The fact that the Lord Jesus Christ was born of a virgin is foundational to the Christian faith.

The faith we demonstrate in our lives is measured by our acceptance of Jesus Christ being both God and man. The apostle Paul makes this very clear: *"But when the fullness of time was come, God sent forth His Son, made of a woman . . ."* (Galatians 4:4). 2 Timothy 3:16 says: *"Without controversy great is the mystery of godliness: God was manifest in the flesh . . ."*

CLOSING THOUGHTS

The Lord honored Mary above any other woman in history by choosing her to be the mother of His Son, Jesus Christ. But we must be careful not to give Mary more honor than we give to God Himself as revealed in His Son, Jesus Christ.

Mary was a channel, a person through whom God brought forth His perfect will. Mary demonstrated purity, humility, faith, and submission to God's plan for her. She was obedient, not even thinking of the cost to her own reputation. Imagine the reaction of the town's people when word got around that Mary was about to be an unwed mother!

We need to remember that God, in the form of the Holy Spirit, lives in our bodies and desires to use us, too. We will not be used in the same way that Mary was, but God does have a perfect plan for each of us. What response do we give God when He wants to use us for His glory? 1 Corinthians 6:19–20 gives us these truths to consider: *"What? know ye not that your body is the temple of the Holy Ghost which is in you, which ye have of God, and ye are not your own? For ye are bought with a price: therefore glorify God in your body, and in your spirit, which are God's."*

FOR DISCUSSION

1. Discuss what is known about Mary's background.
2. What responsibilities did Mary have as the earthly mother of the Lord Jesus?
3. List four qualities evidenced in Mary's life that we should follow.
4. Explain why Mary was only a channel whom God used and is not to be worshiped.
5. How can you let God use you to fulfill His eternal plan?

CHAPTER 36

MARY

MOTHER OF JESUS: PART 2

The Bible records the words *"Blessed among women."* Mary certainly is to be honored, but she was just a woman. She is not to be worshiped as God, although we can follow the example of her life of obedience to God.

Mary's Life

Mary's giving birth to Jesus was the beginning of her work, not the end. She was His mother. Jesus was at home with her for 30 years before He began his public ministry. Never forget this: even though Jesus became man, He still was God. That means He was perfect. Mary could not make Him any more perfect than He was. But the Bible says in Luke 2:51 that Jesus grew up as did the other children in the home, and submitted to Mary and Joseph while He lived with them.

Because of their lowly background, Joseph and Mary could not give Jesus much wealth. Nor could they introduce Him to influential people and upper-class society. They probably could not afford the best education of the day. What then did Mary give to her Son?

First, she gave Him birth. Because no other human was involved with His birth, Jesus may have looked like her. She may have given Him physical characteristics.

Next, she was a faithful wife and mother who gave Jesus a home with loving parents. She married Joseph, a man who worked hard to provide a living for the family. Mary and Joseph had their own children after Jesus was virgin born. From the verses in Matthew 13:55–56, we know that Jesus lived with four half-brothers and at least two half-sisters. Jesus had a secure home filled with a mother's love.

Mary's service to and for her Son—who was also her Savior—is similar to a mother's service to her family today. Mary was a good mother; more than that, she was a godly mother. The question for those of us who are mothers is this: What do we want for our children? Often, concern about material things overshadows the more important godly characteristics we should be passing on to our children.

Mary's Sorrow

It is hard for us to think of Mary as having a sad life. After all, she was chosen by God to be Jesus' mother. She heard the testimony of the shepherds the night of His birth. She saw the wise men from the East bring gifts to Jesus and worship Him. As Jesus grew up, she saw how perfectly He developed physically and spiritually. Luke 2:40 says: *"And the child grew, and waxed strong in spirit, filled with wisdom: and the grace of God was upon him."*

Where did her sorrow come from? Her sorrow was the fulfillment of a prophesy made when Joseph and Mary took Jesus to the temple to present Him to the Lord according to the Law as told in Luke 2:27, 34–35:

> [27] And he came by the Spirit into the temple: and when the parents brought in the child Jesus, to do for him after the custom of the law,
> [34] And Simeon blessed them, and said unto Mary his mother, Behold, this child is set for the fall and rising again of many in Israel; and for a sign which shall be spoken against;
> [35] Yea, a sword shall pierce through thy own soul also, that the thoughts of many hearts may be revealed.

Perhaps the first "piercing of the sword" or sorrow Mary felt happened when Jesus was 12 years old. The verses in Luke 2:43, 46, 49 tell of the event when Jesus stayed on in the temple after Mary and Joseph had started for home:

> [43] And when they had fulfilled the days, as they returned, the child Jesus tarried behind in Jerusalem; and Joseph and his mother knew not of it.
> [46] And it came to pass, that after three days they found him in the temple, sitting in the midst of the doctors, both hearing them, and asking them questions.
> [49] And he said unto them, How is it that ye sought me? wist ye not that I must be about my Father's business?

We can appreciate the heartache Mary must have felt when she realized Jesus was missing. For three days His parents looked for Him. When they did find Him, it must have hurt to hear Jesus say in front of everyone in the temple that He "must be about His Father's business." Even though He returned with them to Nazareth, it still must have been frustrating for them to watch Jesus separate Himself from His earthly family and talk about His heavenly Father.

Then the day came when Jesus left His earthly home to begin His public ministry. We can only imagine that this separation was like the thrust of a sword in Mary's heart.

Mary was asked to bear even greater sorrow. The deepest sorrow that pierced her like a sword came the day Jesus died on the cross. The Bible tells us in John 19:25 that Mary stood beneath the cross. She saw His face beaten beyond human recognition, saw her Son nailed to a cross between two thieves, heard people mocking, and saw a sword thrust in His side.

Even though Jesus had to leave home to carry on His ministry during the last three years of His earthly life, Mary did not forsake her Son. Neither did Jesus forget His mother. In His final moments on the cross, in His own deepest sorrow, Jesus remembered to see that His mother was cared for. We read this in John 19:26–27:

> [26] When Jesus therefore saw his mother, and the disciple standing by, whom he loved, he saith unto his mother, Woman, behold thy son!
>
> [27] Then saith he to the disciple, Behold thy mother! And from that hour that disciple took her unto his own home.

Mary's Need of a Savior

Mary is mentioned again in Acts 1:12–14:

> [12] Then returned they unto Jerusalem from the mount called Olivet, which is from Jerusalem a sabbath day's journey.
>
> [13] And when they were come in, they went up into an upper room, where abode both Peter, and James, and John, and Andrew, Philip, and Thomas, Bartholomew, and Matthew, James the son of Alphaeus, and Simon Zelotes, and Judas the brother of James.
>
> [14] These all continued with one accord in prayer and supplication, with the women, and Mary the mother of Jesus, and with his brethren.

Mary was in the upper room with the disciples and other faithful women, waiting for the coming of the Holy Spirit. She knew her Son was alive, but more importantly, she knew He was her Savior. She was among the first group of Christians, ready to live for God as a devout follower of Christ. It is interesting that her name is given not first, but last in the long list of people gathered. This teaches us that Mary should never be given a place of prominence or be worshiped. Mary's name is not mentioned again in the New Testament, but we do have mention of the apostles who were leaders in the early Church.

Mary was not sinless. She recognized her need of deliverance from sin when she said in Luke 1:47: *"And my spirit hath rejoiced in God **my Saviour.**"*

It is important we clearly understand in this statement that Mary recognized and admitted her own dependence on the Lord Jesus Christ as her personal Savior.

CLOSING THOUGHTS

Before concluding our study of Mary's life, we must consider the words she said at the wedding feast in Cana. When the host fell into the embarrassing position of not having sufficient wine at the feast, Mary spoke to Jesus about the problem. She also instructed the servants with words valuable for us all: *"Whatsoever he saith unto you, do it"* (John 2:5).

Mary recognized that Jesus was the Son of God and His power came from God when she told the servants to do whatever Jesus told them. She demonstrated her faith, knowing and believing Jesus alone could solve this problem. Even though Mary is the human mother of the Lord Jesus, it is evident from the events at this wedding that she had no special power or ability to perform miracles. That power belongs only to God. It was Jesus who turned the water to wine, not Mary.

In a way, Jesus rebuked Mary by saying that His hour was not yet come. If Mary had been in any way supernatural or part of the God-head, as some claim, Jesus would not have spoken to her in this way. By speaking like this to His mother, Jesus shows His authority as being higher than that of Mary.

We must be careful to honor Mary as a woman chosen and blessed by God, but not to give her more authority than God Himself does. Let us do as Mary instructed the servants at the wedding concerning Jesus, *"Whatever He tells you to do, do it."* Let us ask God to help us be obedient, and do what He says.

FOR DISCUSSION

1. Describe the home life Jesus must have had with Mary as His mother.
2. What is the most important responsibility mothers have to their children?
3. Name two ways Jesus' life brought sorrow to Mary.
4. How did Mary prove her love for Jesus even after He left home?
5. What lessons have you learned from the life of Mary?

CHAPTER 37

ELIZABETH

A WOMAN BLAMELESS BEFORE GOD

Elizabeth: Righteous and Blameless

Elizabeth was the wife of Zacharias, a priest, and the mother of John the Baptist. John was sent by God to prepare the way for Jesus Christ. Elizabeth's story is told in Luke 1. Verse 6 says: *"And they were both righteous before God, walking in all the commandments and ordinances of the Lord blameless."* God approved of this couple and the way they lived before Him.

God didn't say they had a perfect home. But He described them as people who were blameless. No matter what our marital status, we need to look at our homes. We need to consider our personal commitment to God and His Word, and see how that affects our daily lives. If God were writing about you, what would He say about your home?

Elizabeth's Disgrace and God's Answer

In spite of Elizabeth's blameless position before the Lord, Luke 1:7 tells us she—like many of us today—had heartaches and disappointments. *"They had no child, because that Elisabeth was barren, and they both were now well stricken in years."* Imagine how often Elizabeth prayed to God for a child. At that time in that culture, it was a disgrace for a woman not to have children. And because Elizabeth was a member of the priestly line and married to a priest, it was even worse for her to be childless. Who would carry on the priesthood?

God sent His angel, Gabriel, to Zacharias while he was carrying out his priestly duties. It is interesting to note how often God moved in mighty ways while His children were doing what they had been told to do. That should be a reminder to us to be busy doing what God wants us to.

God's Promise

The angel told Zacharias that the Lord had heard their prayers. Elizabeth would give birth to a son, and they were to name him John. The angel went on to describe how they were to bring him up, what his job in life would be, and what he was to be named at the time of his birth. Zacharias did not believe the angel, and asked how he could know if this were true. After all, he and his wife were too old to have children.

We can understand Zacharias' thinking, because often we act the same way. We pray for things, sometimes for years, and then when God answers, we can't believe it. Zacharias' questions, however, did not stop God from working out His plan. Zacharias was given the confirmation he wanted; he was unable to speak until the baby was born and named.

The Bible does not tell us Elizabeth's reaction to her husband's inability to speak. She must have believed whatever it was her husband wrote to her. The Bible says that when Zacharias returned home from the temple, Elizabeth conceived and gave praise to God. In Luke 1:25 she said: *"Thus hath the Lord dealt with me in the days wherein he looked on me, to take away my reproach among men."*

Mary's Visit

During her pregnancy, Elizabeth kept herself secluded for five months. In her sixth month, her unmarried young cousin, Mary, came to visit. Mary was also pregnant. The difference between the two women was that Mary was the virgin whom God had chosen to be the mother of His Son, the Messiah. We read this account in Luke 1:39–44:

³⁹ And Mary arose in those days, and went into the hill country with haste, into a city of Juda;

⁴⁰ And entered into the house of Zacharias, and saluted Elisabeth.

⁴¹ And it came to pass, that, when Elisabeth heard the salutation of Mary, the babe leaped in her womb; and Elisabeth was filled with the Holy Ghost:

⁴² And she spake out with a loud voice, and said, Blessed art thou among women, and blessed is the fruit of thy womb.

⁴³ And whence is this to me, that the mother of my Lord should come to me?

⁴⁴ For, lo, as soon as the voice of thy salutation sounded in mine ears, the babe leaped in my womb for joy.

Let's put ourselves in Elizabeth's place. How would we react to a member of our family who was unmarried and pregnant? Whatever Elizabeth's feelings were, she was obedient to the Holy Spirit and knew Mary's baby was a special child. God used Elizabeth to give comfort and reassurance to Mary. Mary might have been afraid of what people would think about her pregnancy. But Elizabeth reached out to help and reassure Mary. Elizabeth was the first woman recorded in the Bible to give a verbal confession that Jesus was indeed the Lord.

Luke 1:56 says that Mary stayed with Elizabeth for about three months. These cousins must have talked about the miracles God had done in their lives. Is it any wonder that after Jesus was born, Mary thought about all these things? She and Elizabeth gained a deep reverence for God's work in their lives.

The Promise Fulfilled

Luke 1:57–64 records the birth of Elizabeth's son:

⁵⁷ Now Elisabeth's full time came that she should be delivered; and she brought forth a son.

⁵⁸ And her neighbours and her cousins heard how the

Lord had shewed great mercy upon her; and they
rejoiced with her.

[59] And it came to pass, that on the eighth day they
came to circumcise the child; and they called him
Zacharias, after the name of his father.

[60] And his mother answered and said, Not so; but
he shall be called John.

[61] And they said unto her, There is none of thy
kindred that is called by this name.

[62] And they made signs to his father, how he would
have him called.

[63] And he asked for a writing table, and wrote, saying,
His name is John. And they marvelled all.

[64] And his mouth was opened immediately, and his
tongue loosed, and he spake, and praised God.

Family and neighbors rejoiced with Zacharias and Elizabeth
at the birth of their son. The couple were well known in their
town, so God received glory as many rejoiced with them.

In spite of Zacharias' inability to talk, he and Elizabeth had
agreed to obey the angel's command to name their son John. This
devotion to each other and obedience to God's instruction was a
testimony to those present at the naming of the baby. Everyone
marveled at their unity.

Their son, called "John," was a unique man who had the
honor of preparing the way for the Messiah. Elizabeth was willing to acknowledge Mary as the one chosen to be the mother of
the Messiah. We find no evidence that Elizabeth thought *she*
should have been chosen since she was older and wiser than
Mary. His mother's humble spirit must have influenced John. We
read John's words about the Lord Jesus Christ: *"He must increase,
but I must decrease"* (John 3:30).

CLOSING THOUGHTS

Let's think for a moment about the type of women we are:

- Are we women others would turn to for comfort, reassurance, and spiritual fellowship as Mary was able to turn to Elizabeth?
- Are we ready to help those around us who are in need or in trouble?
- Are we faithfully doing what God wants us to?
- Do we grumble and complain because of circumstances in our lives?
- Are we ready to believe God when He answers our prayers?

Let us commit our lives to God's control. Then, with His help, let's determine to walk in obedience to His commandments.

FOR DISCUSSION

1. What does it mean to walk blameless before God?
2. In what way was Elizabeth's pregnancy unique?
3. How did Elizabeth help Mary?
4. Why was the timing of Elizabeth's pregnancy significant?
5. What lessons did Zacharias learn from the birth of his son?

CHAPTER 38

ANNA

A WIDOW WHO SERVED GOD

This study is about a prophetess named Anna, one of only two women named in the New Testament who had this title given to her. Other New Testament women were called prophetesses, but are not named.

Anna's Background

The Bible doesn't tell us why Anna was called a prophetess. It does say she was a widow. Perhaps her husband had been a prophet. Or perhaps God gave her special insight into the future. Whatever the reason, the Bible says she was a prophetess, as we read in Luke 2:36–37:

> [36] And there was one Anna, a prophetess, the daughter of Phanuel, of the tribe of Aser: she was of a great age, and had lived with an husband seven years from her virginity;
> [37] And she was a widow of about fourscore and four years, which departed not from the temple, but served God with fastings and prayers night and day.

Anna lived during a time when the Roman Empire dominated the entire Mediterranean world. Its philosophy, wealthy lifestyle, and religious beliefs all opposed the idea of a coming Messiah.

Anna, however, was loyal to God. She worked faithfully in the temple and was not distracted by her environment. She eagerly anticipated the coming of the Messiah to redeem Israel from the rule of Rome. She surely must have heard the prophecies of Christ's birth read over and over again as she worked in the temple.

Isaiah was one of the books of prophecy commonly read in the temple. Anna would have heard predictions concerning Jesus' birth, such as the one in Isaiah 7:14: *"Therefore the Lord himself shall give you a sign; Behold, a virgin shall conceive, and bear a son, and shall call his name Immanuel."*

Anna may also have been familiar with the prophecy in Micah 5:2, where the birthplace of Jesus was foretold: *"But thou, Bethlehem Ephratah, though thou be little among the thousands of Judah, yet out of thee shall he come forth unto me that is to be ruler in Israel; whose goings forth have been from of old, from everlasting."*

Anna's Situation in Life

Anna had been married for seven years when her husband died. She had no children and had been widowed for 84 years when the Bible first mentions her name. She must have been more than 100 years old!

In thinking of people who have blessed my life, I recall a number of older people. I believe one of the greatest gifts the Church has today is its older Christians. People around them can sense the reality of their walk with the Lord. Their faces glow with God's love, and they speak with wisdom. If you are an older person, don't feel you are no longer of use. God continues to need older people in His service.

Anna was a widow; she knew what it meant to be lonely. She could have withdrawn and felt sorry for herself. She could have become depressed. She could have been angry with God for taking her husband when she was so young. But the Bible shows a different picture. Anna was a busy woman, working long hours in the temple of God.

Anna is a good example of 1 Corinthians 4:2: *"Moreover it is required in stewards, that a man be found faithful."* God expects us to be faithful and trustworthy with our material goods, blessings, and abilities in whatever circumstances He places us.

Besides her work in the temple, Anna was a woman who prayed and fasted regularly. She put God's work before her own desires. She was willing to deny herself in order to perform the Lord's work.

Anna Sees the Messiah

One day as Anna entered the temple, God allowed her to see the Messiah with her own eyes. According to the custom of the Jews, Jesus was about 40 days old when Mary and Joseph brought Him to the temple and dedicated Him to God. A godly man named Simeon was the first one in the temple to whom Joseph and Mary presented the infant Jesus.

Just as Simeon was praising the Lord for allowing him to live long enough to see God's own Son, Anna walked in and joined in praise. By faith, she began telling others about God's provision of redemption. The last we read about Anna is in Luke 2:38: *"And she coming in that instant gave thanks likewise unto the Lord, and spake of him to all them that looked for redemption in Jerusalem."*

CLOSING THOUGHTS

What can the life of Anna teach us? We have seen Anna as an elderly widow, a devout worshiper of God, and a prophetess, but I think we can see her in one more way. The final words in the Bible about her say she told everyone about the Messiah's coming. She was a witness to the redemption found in Christ Jesus. After all the years of waiting, praying, and fasting, Anna had the joy of telling about the Redeemer's arrival.

How often—if ever—do we women take time in our busy lives to eagerly anticipate Christ's second coming? The apostle John wrote these words as a prayer: *"Even so, come, Lord Jesus"* (Revelation 22:20). When was the last time any of us prayed for the Lord Jesus to return? Are we bold in telling those around us that Jesus has come once and will come again?

Anna did not indulge in self-pity. Depression and self-pity seem common temptations for women. We need to rise above these and occupy ourselves with God's work. Like Anna, we should be faithful in prayer, knowledgeable in the Scriptures, and busy in God's work. For 84 years, Anna had heard the prophecies read in the temple. She knew what God's Word said and looked for the coming of Messiah in keeping with that Word. Like Anna, we should anticipate the second coming of Messiah. Hebrews 9:28 says: *"So Christ was once offered to bear the sins of many; and unto them that look for him shall he appear the second time without sin unto salvation."*

As we close this study, let us pause a few minutes and pray. Praise the Lord for His blessings, then work and live as if you fully expect to see the Lord's return in your lifetime. It may even be today!

FOR DISCUSSION

1. Describe the time period in which Anna lived.
2. With what activities did Anna fill her days?
3. What was Anna's reaction to seeing the Messiah?
4. How can we live in anticipation of Jesus' Second Coming?
5. In what three ways can Anna's life be an example to us?

CHAPTER 39

SALOME

A WOMAN WHO PRAYED FOR HER SONS

For the remaining lessons from the New Testament, we will list the life accounts of the women in the order they appear in the Bible. That is not always the same as the chronological time period in which the events happened, but it is a convenient way to find the stories in the Bible.

The woman we will study in this chapter is Salome. She was the wife of Zebedee and the mother of James and John, two of Jesus' twelve apostles.

Her Family

Zebedee, Salome's husband, was a successful fisherman who had hired servants. When Jesus first saw him, he was busy mending fishing nets with his two sons. Jesus called to his sons and asked them to follow Him. Apparently Zebedee did not hesitate to let his sons go. The gospel of Mark tells us, *"And straightway he called them: and they left their father Zebedee in the ship with the hired servants, and went after him"* (Mark 1:20). James and John left all they were familiar with to follow Jesus.

Although the Bible does not say much about Zebedee and Salome's home life, we know Salome was one of the women who followed Jesus and helped serve Him. James and John saw an example in their parents' lives which they could follow. It would seem that Zebedee and Salome taught their children the Scriptures and believed in the coming Messiah. They were united in their love for God and their willingness to let their sons leave the family business to follow the Lord Jesus. They did not know when—or if—James and John would return home.

A Follower of Jesus

Looking at another passage in the Bible, we find Salome with a group of women at the crucifixion of Jesus. At the darkest hour of Jesus' life, when even His disciples, including Salome's own sons, had withdrawn from Him, women watched Jesus from a distance. Salome was among those women, as Mark 15:40–41 describes:

> [40] There were also women looking on afar off: among whom was Mary Magdalene, and Mary the mother of James the less and of Joses, and Salome;
> [41] (Who also, when he was in Galilee, followed him, and ministered unto him;) and many other women which came up with him unto Jerusalem.

In Mark 16, Salome is included in the group of women who anointed the body of Jesus. She was there during the darkness of the crucifixion, but she was also present on the glorious Resurrection morning. Mark 16:1–2, 5–7 records that it was women who first heard the good news that Jesus had arisen from the dead:

> [1] And when the sabbath was past, Mary Magdalene, and Mary the mother of James, and Salome, had bought sweet spices, that they might come and anoint him.
> [2] And very early in the morning the first day of the week, they came unto the sepulchre at the rising of the sun.
> [5] And entering into the sepulchre, they saw a young man sitting on the right side, clothed in a long white garment; and they were affrighted.

⁶ And he saith unto them, Be not affrighted: Ye seek Jesus of Nazareth, which was crucified: he is risen; he is not here: behold the place where they laid him.

⁷ But go your way, tell his disciples and Peter that he goeth before you into Galilee: there shall ye see him, as he said unto you.

Her Ambition

Salome was devoted to Jesus and recognized Him as the Messiah. She believed Jesus would one day come into power in an earthly kingdom. Like other mothers, she was ambitious for her sons. She knew they were close to Jesus, so she boldly requested that her sons be given a place of honor in His kingdom. She asked that one son sit on His left side and the other on His right side when He sat on His throne, places reserved for the second and third rulers in a kingdom. Here is what Salome said, as we read in Matthew 20:20–23:

²⁰ Then came to him the mother of Zebedee's children with her sons, worshipping him, and desiring a certain thing of him.

²¹ And he (Jesus) said unto her, What wilt thou? She saith unto him, Grant that these my two sons may sit, the one on thy right hand, and the other on the left, in thy kingdom.

²² But Jesus answered and said, Ye know not what ye ask. Are ye able to drink of the cup that I shall drink of, and to be baptized with the baptism that I am baptized with? They say unto him, We are able.

²³ And he saith unto them, Ye shall drink indeed of my cup, and be baptized with the baptism that I am baptized with: but to sit on my right hand, and on my left, is not mine to give, but it shall be given to them for whom it is prepared of my Father.

This unusual request from Salome stemmed from maternal pride and a desire for the best for her sons. She did not realize that suffering was to be a major part of the kingdom. Jesus rebuked her misguided ambition and corrected her misunderstanding of what her request included. He answered her in a way that neither Salome nor her sons were expecting. Jesus simply told them that to be near Him on His throne also meant they would have to share in His sufferings.

History tells us that both James and John did indeed share in Christ's suffering. It is believed that James was the first apostle martyred, and John, who outlived the rest, was exiled to the island of Patmos.

As Salome and her sons followed Jesus, I am sure they learned much. From this one incident we see how Jesus taught them the concept of who was great in God's kingdom. Matthew 20:25–27 reads:

> [25] But Jesus called them unto him, and said, Ye know that the princes of the Gentiles exercise dominion over them, and they that are great exercise authority upon them.
>
> [26] But it shall not be so among you: but whosoever will be great among you, let him be your minister;
>
> [27] And whosoever will be chief among you, let him be your servant.

CLOSING THOUGHTS

We need to be careful in criticizing Salome's request for her sons. Keep in mind the positive lessons she taught them. We must learn to appreciate the full extent to which a godly life can influence our children. Often it is because of a mother's prayers and consistent testimony that children surrender their lives to God at a young age.

When children become teenagers, the faith in God they

observe in the example of godly parents is a potent antidote against sin. No happiness can be compared to that of Christian parents who live long enough to see their children living for the glory of God and dedicated to the service of God. Because Salome loved the Lord, her joy must have overflowed because both of her sons became disciples of Jesus and followed Him faithfully until the end of their lives.

We can learn something from Salome. She came to Jesus with a request she should not have made. In a similar way, we sometimes ask God for things we should not. It is not always easy to know what to ask for. John gives us some guidelines in 1 John 3:21–22: *"Beloved, if our heart condemn us not, then have we confidence toward God. And whatsoever we ask, we receive of him, because we keep his commandments, and do those things that are pleasing in his sight."*

If we keep the commandments of the Lord and do those things that are pleasing to Him, we can have confidence when we pray. If we are living for Him, God Himself will lead us in our prayer life. We will find ourselves asking according to His will because we are living according to His will. Then, if we pray for something we should not ask for, the Holy Spirit will let us know that we are asking amiss, much as Jesus let Salome know that her request was not in order. Let us ask God to help us to be women who pray according to His will.

FOR DISCUSSION

1. What example of godly living did Salome show her sons?
2. Name two major events that occurred in Jesus' life when Salome was present.
3. Why do you think she requested places of honor for her sons?
4. What didn't she understand?
5. List three lessons you can learn from the life of Salome.

CHAPTER 40

A WOMAN WITH AN ISSUE OF BLOOD

SHE MET THE GREAT PHYSICIAN

We often take our strong, healthy bodies for granted. When was the last time you thanked God for your health? Although I have often been sick, I appreciate feeling well. Perhaps that is why I feel close to women in the Bible who suffered physically.

The Woman with a Hemorrhage

Today's Bible study is about a woman who had been bleeding for 12 years. She had visited many doctors, but none could help her. To make matters worse, searching for treatment had cost her a lot of money.

Then one day, everything changed; she met Jesus. He not only healed her, but also publicly commended her for her faith.

Background of This Story

Can you picture this woman? She probably looked weak, tired, pale, and discouraged. Most likely, she was poorly dressed since she had spent so much money on treatment.

The first four books in the New Testament—the Gospels—tell us of the life and ministry of Jesus Christ while He lived on Earth. The story we are looking at today is told in three of the Gospels: Matthew, Mark, and Luke.

Not only did Jesus change this woman's life, but also Jesus' treatment of her problem left quite an impression on His disciples. The Bible describes her situation in Mark 5:25–26:

> [25] And a certain woman, which had an issue of blood twelve years,
>
> [26] And had suffered many things of many physicians, and had spent all that she had, and was nothing bettered, but rather grew worse.

Even Luke, the physician, in his account of the story, admits doctors could not heal her (Luke 8:43). It is hard for a doctor to realize there is nothing medicine can do to heal a sick person.

In Leviticus 15:19–33 we read the laws God gave the Israelites concerning what women could and could not do when they were bleeding, whether it was their normal monthly menstruation, a postpartum situation, or a gynecological condition in which bleeding persisted. The latter seems to be the case with the woman in this story. A woman in such condition was considered unclean and outcast from the rest of society until she could be declared clean once again.

In Romans 6:14, Paul says, *"For ye are not under the law, but under grace."* Jesus demonstrated the truth of that verse by showing this woman grace. He did not punish her for disobeying the Old Testament law, which forbade her to be in public or to touch someone else's clothing.

Women today take comfort from knowing they do not have to stay isolated or outcast from other Christians or their families because of biological or medical conditions which result in bleeding. During menstruation, following childbirth, or at any other time in her life, a woman is free to take communion, serve God, and fellowship in the church.

Her Remarkable Faith

Since this woman was considered unclean and treated as an outcast, it is amazing she even had the courage to approach Jesus in a crowd of people. Her faith was outstanding. She seemed driven with a single thought and purpose: she wanted only to be able to get close enough to Jesus to touch His clothes. This not only showed her faith, but her tremendous humility. We read the rest of the story in Mark 5:27–34:

> [27] When she had heard of Jesus, came in the press behind, and touched his garment.
>
> [28] For she said, If I may touch but his clothes, I shall be whole.
>
> [29] And straightway the fountain of her blood was dried up; and she felt in her body that she was healed of that plague.
>
> [30] And Jesus, immediately knowing in himself that virtue had gone out of him, turned him about in the press, and said, Who touched my clothes?
>
> [31] And his disciples said unto him, Thou seest the multitude thronging thee, and sayest thou, Who touched me?
>
> [32] And he looked round about to see her that had done this thing.
>
> [33] But the woman fearing and trembling, knowing what was done in her, came and fell down before him, and told him all the truth.
>
> [34] And he said unto her, Daughter, thy faith hath made thee whole; go in peace, and be whole of thy plague.

How Jesus Healed Her

It is interesting that Jesus called her "daughter." Perhaps this was because she was a daughter of Abraham, meaning a spiritual descendant of Abraham. But it is also a term used when we want someone to feel as though they belong to our family and are important to us. I think Jesus shows compassion by using this term.

When Jesus said, *"Be whole"* or *"Be healed,"* those words must have brought peace and joy to this woman. Imagine the difference in what Jesus said compared to what doctors had told her. The Bible indicates she was healed immediately when she touched His garment, even before He spoke to her.

By this time, the crowd following Jesus wondered what was going on. In the midst of masses of people, Jesus asked who touched Him! Even the disciples couldn't believe the question.

Perhaps Jesus wanted the woman to publicly confess her faith in Him. She showed courage coming into the crowd to get to Jesus. But she showed even greater courage by admitting she was the one who had touched Jesus' clothes and by openly bowing at His feet.

The Bible says the woman told Jesus her history. Of course, Jesus knew all about her. Still, He patiently listened. The Lord Jesus wants to hear us tell Him our concerns, even though He already knows them.

Jesus Has Time for Compassion

Another amazing aspect of this account is the fact that Jesus was on His way to heal another person—Jairus' young daughter. Even with His mind on where He was going, Jesus was sensitive to the needs of this woman. He had time for compassion then; He has time to be compassionate to us, too.

Mark 5:32 says Jesus knew who the woman was as He looked at her. Naturally she was afraid. She had tried to do something quietly and unnoticed. But Jesus made her situation public. Perhaps He wanted everyone in the crowd to know she was now clean and could live among them again. The Lord told her to go in peace.

CLOSING THOUGHTS

The Bible clearly states it was the woman's faith that healed her. She was not healed because she touched Jesus' robes. Some people have a mistaken concept. They think that if they can just touch a "sacred" object or drink "holy" water, God will perform a miracle. Ephesians 2:8–9 makes it clear that our salvation does not come about because of any good works we do. Neither do we receive any merit or special benefit because of what we ourselves do: *"For by grace are ye saved through faith; and that not of yourselves: it is the gift of God: Not of works, lest any man should boast."*

The woman was healed because she had faith in the Lord Jesus Christ. Hebrews 11:6 says: *"without faith it is impossible to please Him."*

Think about yourself for a moment. When God looks at you, does He see your faith? Can you be open and honest before God like this woman was? I hope so. Then you, too, will see God work mightily in your life.

FOR DISCUSSION

1. Name three characteristics this woman displayed in her life.
2. Name three characteristics the Lord Jesus displayed.
3. Why do you think Jesus made this private encounter so public?
4. What was it that healed this woman's condition: her faith, Jesus' words, or touching His garment?
5. This story is told to us in three of the four Gospels. Why do you think it is repeated?

CHAPTER 41

SYROPHOENICIAN WOMAN

SHE SHOWED GREAT FAITH

In this lesson we will look at another woman who had great faith. Because of her persistent faith in asking Jesus for something, she received a wonderful answer to a major problem in her life. This story reminds me that God does hear my prayers even if it seems His answer is "No."

Background

Just before this event took place, Jesus had fed a multitude of 5,000 people. Then the Lord went alone to a mountain to pray. While He was there, His disciples crossed the lake in a boat. A storm blew up and the disciples needed help. Just then, Jesus walked to them on the water.

As Jesus and His disciples got out of the boat on the other side of the lake, crowds suffering with all kinds of sicknesses were waiting for Jesus. He and His disciples were tired and weary. The Pharisees asked Jesus questions, trying to find a reason to accuse Him. At this point, Jesus decided to withdraw from the crowds. He wanted no one to know where He was.

He went to an area called Tyre and Sidon, a Gentile district north of Galilee, where this story takes place. We can read about it in the gospels of both Matthew and Mark.

The Woman Comes to Jesus

Mark 7:24–26 tells us the first part of the story:

> [24] And from thence he arose, and went into the borders of Tyre and Sidon, and entered into an house, and would have no man know it: but he could not be hid.
>
> [25] For a certain woman, whose young daughter had an unclean spirit, heard of him, and came and fell at his feet:
>
> [26] The woman was a Greek, a Syrophenician by nation; and she besought him that he would cast forth the devil out of her daughter.

When we are introduced to this woman, our first image is that of a concerned mother. Let us put ourselves in her place. Imagine the heartache and physical fatigue she must have experienced in taking care of her daughter.

Jesus' earthly ministry focused primarily on the Jewish people. John 1:11 tells us, *"He came unto His own."* To the woman whose daughter was ill, it made no difference that she was Greek by race and language. She heard what Jesus had done for others and went to Him for help. She was so concerned for her daughter that she took no thought of the fact that she was a Gentile and Jesus a Jew. Out of a mother's love, she went boldly to Him and laid her request before Him.

Her Talk with Jesus

Her conversation with Jesus is recorded in Matthew 15: 22–28:

> [22] And, behold, a woman of Canaan came out of the same coasts, and cried unto him, saying, Have mercy on me, O Lord, thou Son of David; my daughter is grievously vexed with a devil.
>
> [23] But he answered her not a word. And his disciples came and besought him, saying, Send her away; for she crieth after us.

²⁴ But he answered and said, I am not sent but unto the lost sheep of the house of Israel.

²⁵ Then came she and worshipped him, saying, Lord, help me.

²⁶ But he answered and said, It is not meet to take the children's bread, and to cast it to dogs.

²⁷ And she said, Truth, Lord: yet the dogs eat of the crumbs which fall from their masters' table.

²⁸ Then Jesus answered and said unto her, O woman, great is thy faith: be it unto thee even as thou wilt. And her daughter was made whole from that very hour.

Recognizing Her Place

After this mother presented her plea, Jesus seemed to ignore her. She obviously aggravated the disciples; they wanted Jesus to send her away. But Jesus did not. He eventually answered her by saying that it was not right to take bread from children in order to give it to dogs. In saying this, Jesus meant she had no right as a Gentile to take blessings intended for the Jews. The woman had to understand that before Jesus could help her.

We cannot help but be impressed with the perseverance this woman showed. No matter what Jesus said, she was not discouraged, nor did she lose faith. She agreed with Jesus and asked for only a crumb. In doing so, she acknowledged she wasn't entitled to have what she asked for. Yet she requested that her child be healed.

At this point, she was victorious. Jesus recognized her faith and healed her daughter. He did not even go to where the girl was; He simply spoke and the girl was healed. The woman believed Jesus had performed this miracle.

Her Child Delivered

Mark adds this last detail at the conclusion of the account in Mark 7:30: *"And when she was come to her house, she found the devil gone out, and her daughter laid upon the bed."*

Imagine how happy that mother must have been when she returned home and found her daughter completely healed and peacefully lying in bed. The woman learned a valuable lesson which we, too, need to learn. If we ask in faith, we can expect to see God answer out of His mercy and power.

Surely the woman's faith grew, and she must have shared her news with others in her community. This may have made way for the early Church in Tyre. We read in the book of Acts that later, when Paul came to this area, there were already Christians there who ministered to him (Acts 21:2–5).

CLOSING THOUGHTS

We can learn several things from the woman's plea to Jesus that apply to us when we come to the Lord in prayer.

First she said, "Have mercy on me." Like this woman, we, too, must recognize that we are totally dependent on God's mercy. We often forget this. We somehow think God owes us something, or that we deserve His help. Instead, we must humble ourselves before God and recognize that we are totally dependent on His mercy.

Second, she recognized and acknowledged out loud who Jesus is. She called Him "Lord," and even added "Son of David." She knew He was the God of the Jews. She gave Him His rightful place, yet she knew He was the only one who could help her with her problem.

When we pray, we, too, need to worship the Lord with the words of our mouth by letting Him know we understand who He is. We don't deserve to be included in His blessings. But, through His grace, we are His people when we trust in and receive the Lord Jesus as Savior. Salvation opens the way for us to receive the blessings of God.

Third, the woman got right to the point of her request. She did not use flowery language, memorized prayers, or needless words. She simply stated her request.

God knows about our problems before we pray to Him. But He desires to see our faith, our needs, and our heart's attitude as we seek His help.

Let us be encouraged by the faith shown by this Syrophoenician woman when she came to Jesus. Our God is faithful. He hears the requests of people everywhere who trust in Jesus Christ, no matter who they are.

FOR DISCUSSION

1. What was the physical condition of Jesus and His disciples when this woman came to Him?
2. What was wrong with the Syrophoenician woman's daughter?
3. Why was this woman considered ineligible to receive an answer to her prayer?
4. Name three ways this mother's plea can teach us about prayer.
5. How was this woman's faith evidenced in her life?

CHAPTER 42

AN UNNAMED WOMAN

KNOWN AS "A SINNER"

The woman in this Bible study lived in circumstances so different from most of us that we may find it hard to understand. The Bible does not give her name; she is simply called "a sinner."

Each of the four Gospels approaches the life and ministry of Christ from a different point of view. Often the stories are found in more than one Gospel, but this account is recorded only in Luke.

Setting and Background

Just prior to the beginning of this story, Jesus raised a widow's son from the dead in a city called Nain. A large crowd of people was following Him.

As Jesus and His disciples traveled through Judea, reports of His miracles spread everywhere. John the Baptist was in prison, and the reports even reached him. John sent two men to Jesus to ask if He was truly the Messiah.

Jesus told the men to tell John that *"The blind see, the lame walk, the lepers are cleansed, the deaf hear, the dead are raised, to the poor the gospel is preached"* (Luke 7:22).

Luke goes on to record: *"The Pharisees and lawyers rejected the counsel of God"* (Luke 7:30). One Pharisee named Simon, however, invited Jesus to his house to eat. The Bible does not say why he did this. Maybe he wanted to question Jesus. Or maybe he was curious as to what Jesus would do. Jesus accepted the invitation and went to Simon's house.

A Sinful Woman Comes to Jesus

While Jesus was in Simon's house, the woman who is called "a sinner" came to see Him. We read about this in Luke 7:36–39:

> [36] And one of the Pharisees desired him that he would eat with him. And he went into the Pharisee's house, and sat down to meat.
>
> [37] And, behold, a woman in the city, which was a sinner, when she knew that Jesus sat at meat in the Pharisee's house, brought an alabaster box of ointment,
>
> [38] And stood at his feet behind him weeping, and began to wash his feet with tears, and did wipe them with the hairs of her head, and kissed his feet, and anointed them with the ointment.
>
> [39] Now when the Pharisee which had bidden him saw it, he spake within himself, saying, This man, if he were a prophet, would have known who and what manner of woman this is that toucheth him: for she is a sinner.

Everyone since Eve—the first person to sin—has been born with a sin nature. Besides that, each of us has sinned enough in our own lives to be called a sinner. Nevertheless, the woman who came to Jesus in Simon's house has the distinguishing label of being called "a sinner." She seems to have been marked publicly as an especially bad person.

Simon Surprised at Jesus

Simon's reaction of shock further shows how deeply engrossed the woman was in the sin she practiced. Simon could not believe that a good person like Jesus would associate with such a sinful woman. Not only did she come to see Jesus, she also brought a gift and repented of her sins, weeping. She came to Jesus for help and He accepted her gift, forgave her sins, and accepted her worship.

Why was this so hard for Simon to understand? The answer is that Simon had not yet accepted the fact that Jesus was the Messiah. He did not realize that Jesus came to Earth to seek out and save sinners. Simon also did not understand the meaning of forgiveness. He had no idea of the importance of showing repentance. Jesus, knowing Simon's heart, told him a story to illustrate love and forgiveness. We find this story in Luke 7:41–43, 47:

41 There was a certain creditor which had two debtors: the one owed five hundred pence, and the other fifty.

42 And when they had nothing to pay, he frankly forgave them both. Tell me therefore, which of them will love him most?

43 Simon answered and said, I suppose that he, to whom he forgave most. And he said unto him, Thou hast rightly judged.

47 Wherefore I say unto thee, Her sins, which are many, are forgiven; for she loved much: but to whom little is forgiven, the same loveth little.

We don't know what Simon did after he heard Jesus' story. But surely his understanding of God's forgiveness increased.

The Sinful Woman's Repentance

What about the woman herself? What did she do and what did Jesus tell her? We need to look closely at her repentance.

The Bible says she brought an alabaster box of ointment and anointed Jesus' feet. He did not refuse this token of her love. She shed tears on His feet, then wiped them with her own hair.

Imagine the scene. Her guilt caused her grief as she entered Jesus' presence. Jesus let her grieve and show her love, then He accepted her worship. We could learn better to forgive ourselves if we would first grieve for our sins, then accept the forgiveness of the Lord in the way this woman did.

The woman's sobs and tenderness of heart show she had a sympathetic spirit. Her sinful lifestyle had not hardened her beyond tears. She had not grown cold and unfeeling.

As the woman heard Jesus defend her acts of devotion and repentance in front of Simon, she must have been in awe. We see Christ's final words to her in Luke 7:48, 50:

> [48] And he said unto her, Thy sins are forgiven.
> [50] And he said to the woman, Thy faith hath saved thee; go in peace.

The Now Righteous Woman's Peace

As Jesus spoke to her, any lingering fear in her heart as to whether she had been forgiven totally vanished. His words, "Go in peace," gave her a whole new life. 2 Corinthians 5:17 gives this assurance: *"If anyone be in Christ, he is a new creation; old things are passed away; behold all things become new."* The Prince of Peace offered this sinful woman peace. She accepted His offer and received God's peace.

Again, we must realize it was the woman's faith that saved her, not her tears and acts of love. Her sins were forgiven because of her faith in the only One who could forgive her sins.

CLOSING THOUGHTS

Maybe like this woman you, too, need to ask Jesus for forgiveness. Let me encourage you to turn from your sins and receive Him as your personal Savior.

If, on the other hand, you are like Simon the Pharisee, you need to ask God to help you understand forgiveness. Simon looked down on the woman because of her sinful lifestyle, so it was hard for him to understand complete forgiveness. We need to ask ourselves if we are willing to witness to those we consider deeply engrossed in sin. What is our reaction when such people tell us they want to talk about repentance or actually do repent of their sin?

Jesus allowed this woman to show her repentance. Then He forgave her sins. He also taught the Pharisee Simon about forgiveness. As believers in Jesus Christ, we are to become more and more like our Lord. In order to be like Christ, we need to learn and apply in our lives both of these lessons: repentance for our own sins and forgiveness of others who sin.

FOR DISCUSSION
1. How did the Pharisees react to Jesus' teaching?
2. Describe what this woman did when she came into Simon's house.
3. Why was it so hard for Simon to understand Jesus' reaction to this woman?
4. What important lessons did Jesus teach through this story?
5. Name one way your life could improve from the lessons in this story.

CHAPTER 43

MARTHA

A WOMAN GIVEN TO HOSPITALITY

In this study and the next, we will look at Martha and Mary, who lived in Bethany. Studies about these sisters often point out the differences between them, leaving the impression that one is better than the other. We will look at each one separately to see what good traits we can learn from each of them.

Martha's Home

The Bible gives no history of Martha except to say that she was the sister of Mary and Lazarus. Scripture mentions another man named Lazarus. This Lazarus was the man whom Jesus raised from the dead after he had been buried for four days. Because that account took place at Martha's home, some people believe she was the elder sister. She certainly took responsibility for acting as hostess. One Bible story found in Luke 10:38–42 clearly shows Martha's character:

[38] Now it came to pass, as they went, that he entered into a certain village: and a certain woman named Martha received him into her house.

[39] And she had a sister called Mary, which also sat at Jesus' feet, and heard his word.

[40] But Martha was cumbered about much serving, and came to him, and said, Lord, dost thou not care that my sister hath left me to serve alone? bid her therefore that she help me.

⁴¹ And Jesus answered and said unto her, Martha,
Martha, thou art careful and troubled about many
things:

⁴² But one thing is needful: and Mary hath chosen
that good part, which shall not be taken away from her.

After Jesus began His public ministry, He did not often
return to His own home in Nazareth for rest and relaxation.
Instead, He went to this home in Bethany. He received a warm
welcome there, and He loved Martha, Mary, and Lazarus.

The Bible describes Martha as a beautiful example of a hostess. Jesus traveled with His disciples and other followers, so at
least 13 people arrived at Martha's home, and she graciously
served them all.

Studying the life of Martha leads us to ask ourselves several
questions: How would I react if 13 or more people appeared at
my front door for meals and lodging? Is my home clean and
attractive? Do people who come to my home find an inviting
atmosphere that welcomes them? Most of us would not be able
to receive so many people, especially unexpectedly, but the Bible
teaches that we should be ready to show hospitality when we
can.

Martha's Problem

Even though Martha willingly welcomed people into her
home, she became deeply involved in preparing and serving the
meal. While Martha worked, Mary sat at Jesus' feet listening to
Him teach. Martha needed help, but she did not call Mary.
Instead she went to Jesus and told Him to tell Mary to help her.
Martha voiced her anger and frustration in the form of a complaint.

Jesus corrected Martha kindly and lovingly. But since He
repeated her name twice, we know Jesus was serious. Martha is
the only woman Jesus spoke to in this way. He did not correct
her for doing her work; He knew she wanted everything to be

just right for Him and for the disciples. He did correct her, however, because she was too concerned about outward things. This hindered her spiritual and personal communion with Him. Jesus said that Mary had made a better choice, and because she had chosen communion with Him, that would not be taken from her.

Martha spent too much time in preparation. She may have been preparing an elaborate meal, when a simpler one was sufficient. With the time she could have saved, she could also have learned from Jesus. We need to be careful we don't get so busy doing good that we neglect to spend enough time with the Lord in prayer and in the study of Scripture.

Martha's Profession of Faith

The gospel of John records another episode in Martha's life. When Lazarus, her brother, died, the family was engulfed in sorrow. The sisters sent for Jesus to come to heal their brother. But Jesus did not come immediately, and Lazarus died. Scripture tells us that Jesus waited two days after hearing that Lazarus was sick (John 11:6).

When Jesus did arrive, Martha went to meet Him. She said: *"Lord, if thou hadst been here, my brother had not died"* (John 11:21). Then Martha continued, *"But I know, that even now, whatsoever thou wilt ask of God, God will give it thee"* (John 11:22). Notice Martha's faith and confidence in the power of Jesus. Before Jesus entered the house, He and Martha had a conversation about the Resurrection as found in John 11:23–27:

[23] Jesus saith unto her, Thy brother shall rise again.

[24] Martha saith unto him, I know that he shall rise again in the resurrection at the last day.

[25] Jesus said unto her, I am the resurrection, and the life: he that believeth in me, though he were dead, yet shall he live:

[26] And whosoever liveth and believeth in me shall never die. Believest thou this?

[27] She saith unto him, Yea, Lord: I believe that thou art the Christ, the Son of God, which should come into the world.

These verses show that Martha had learned her lesson. She left her work and went to meet Jesus. Immediately she received comfort in her sorrow. Jesus turned her attention away from her grief to Himself. He said, *"I am the resurrection and the life."* He declared His deity, power, and authority. What was true then is true today: the only way to have eternal life is to believe in the Lord Jesus Christ.

Even though Martha may not have understood all Jesus said when He asked if she believed, she gave a clear confession of her faith in Him. Each one of us MUST make a personal profession of faith in Jesus Christ in order to receive the salvation He provided when He died on the Cross for our sins. Romans 10:9 says: *"If thou shalt confess with thy mouth the Lord Jesus, and shalt believe in thine heart that God hath raised him from the dead, thou shalt be saved."* If you have never believed and received Jesus as Savior, won't you do so right now?

Martha's Changed Attitude

The last time Martha is mentioned in the Bible is in John 12:1–11. The setting is a supper in her home, a few days before Passover. Jesus is there with Lazarus. As usual, Martha was busy serving. However, this time there seems to be a sense of peace and calm. During this meal, her sister Mary anointed the feet of Jesus with an expensive ointment. But we hear no complaints from Martha.

CLOSING THOUGHTS

One of the most important things we learn from this study is that Martha opened her home to Jesus. Perhaps the first few times He came, she did not understand who He was. But she still welcomed Him.

Most people know very little about Jesus when they first ask Him into their lives. How do they learn? The same way we learn more about anyone. We must spend time with a person. We must spend time with Jesus reading His Word and talking with Him in prayer.

Martha teaches us that there is danger in being too busy to continue to grow in our relationship with the Lord. Time spent with Jesus and time spent in serving are both important, but they need to be kept in proper balance.

In the next lesson, we will look at Martha's sister, Mary. Like Martha she has much to teach us. Even though these sisters were different, God used them both. It is good to know there is room for each of us in God's family.

FOR DISCUSSION

1. In what ways did Martha set examples of both a good and a poor hostess?
2. Is it ever wrong to work hard for Jesus?
3. Describe the way Jesus corrected Martha. How is this an example to us?
4. When and how did Martha show that she had learned the balance between service and devotion?
5. In what ways can you use your home for the Lord?

CHAPTER 44

MARY

SHE DID WHAT SHE COULD

In the last chapter we began a two-part series on the sisters named Martha and Mary. They lived in Bethany, outside of Jerusalem, with their brother, Lazarus. They loved the Lord, and Martha's home was a place where Jesus liked to visit and rest.

Mary's Desire to Learn

As we study Mary's life, we see she was not like Martha, who was busy with many activities. Mary had a quiet nature. Although they were different, each of them loved and served Jesus in her own way.

While reading about Martha in Luke 10, we also read about Mary. In verse 39, we find her sitting at the feet of Jesus, where she heard His Word. In other examples in the Bible, we see her at the feet of Jesus because she wanted to hear what He was saying. Mary gives us a great example of humility.

Remember Jesus' words in Luke 10:42, *"One thing is needful: and Mary hath chosen that good part, which shall not be taken away from her."* What was that good part? It is the quiet time we spend with the Lord in Bible study and prayer. The "good part" is what the Lord teaches us when we spend time alone with Him. The truths learned at Jesus' feet can never be taken away.

Mary wanted to learn from Jesus. What about us? Are we hungry for spiritual food? What do we do to satisfy our spiritual hunger? Do we take time to listen to what Jesus tells us in His Word? Mary understood the importance of His teaching in her life. In the Sermon on the Mount, Jesus promised: *"Blessed are they which do hunger and thirst after righteousness: for they shall be filled"* (Matthew 5:6). Jesus is the only way to satisfy our hunger for spiritual food.

Mary's Sorrow

How did Mary handle grief in her life? We see the difference in the sisters again when Lazarus died. Martha went out to meet Jesus while He was still on His way to their house. Mary stayed quietly at home. After Jesus comforted Martha, she went back to tell Mary that Jesus had come and was calling for her. Mary immediately went to meet Him. John 11:28–36 gives the following account:

> [28] And when she had so said, she went her way, and called Mary her sister secretly, saying, The Master is come, and calleth for thee.

> [29] As soon as she heard that, she arose quickly, and came unto him.

> [30] Now Jesus was not yet come into the town, but was in that place where Martha met him.

> [31] The Jews then which were with her in the house, and comforted her, when they saw Mary, that she rose up hastily and went out, followed her, saying, She goeth unto the grave to weep there.

> [32] Then when Mary was come where Jesus was, and saw him, she fell down at his feet, saying unto him, Lord, if thou hadst been here, my brother had not died.

> [33] When Jesus therefore saw her weeping, and the Jews also weeping which came with her, he groaned in the spirit, and was troubled,

> [34] And said, Where have ye laid him? They said unto him, Lord, come and see.

> [35] Jesus wept.

> [36] Then said the Jews, Behold how he loved him!

I am sure both sisters loved their brother and sorrowed at his death. But we are told only about Mary's tears. When Jesus saw her tears and broken heart, He wept too. Mary was able to see Jesus' humanity as He shared her grief and tears.

John 11:31 tells about the Jews who were in the house with Mary to comfort her. Mary and Martha had people around them who loved and cared enough for them to share their sadness. The women were known in their community. Because of their previous witness before these people, Mary and Martha now were able to share the miracle of Jesus raising Lazarus from the dead. John 11:45 says: *"Then many of the Jews which came to Mary, and had seen the things which Jesus did, believed on him."*

Even in the dark hours following their brother's death, their home was still open. They could have closed the doors and chosen to be alone. I believe God honored their testimony, and, because of them, others believed.

She Did What She Could

Several days later there was a feast at the home of Mary, Martha, and Lazarus. Jesus and the disciples were there. John 12:2–3 states:

> ² There they made him a supper; and Martha served: but Lazarus was one of them that sat at the table with him.
>
> ³ Then took Mary a pound of ointment of spikenard, very costly, and anointed the feet of Jesus, and wiped his feet with her hair: and the house was filled with the odour of the ointment.

When the smell of the perfume spread throughout the house some people criticized Mary. Judas Iscariot, who later betrayed Jesus, said pouring out that ointment was a waste of money. But how did Jesus react? John 12:7–8 tell us:

> ⁷ Then said Jesus, Let her alone: against the day of my burying hath she kept this.

⁸ For the poor always ye have with you; but me ye have not always.

Mark 14:8–9 expands upon Jesus' words:

⁸ She hath done what she could: she is come afore-hand to anoint my body to the burying.
⁹ Verily I say unto you, Wheresoever this gospel shall be preached throughout the whole world, this also that she hath done shall be spoken of for a memorial of her.

Jesus taught the disciples about His approaching death and burial. Mary likely had heard His teaching and saved the ointment to anoint His body. Now she brought it out and poured it on His feet while He was still alive. Jesus was able to enjoy the fragrance. How sweet it must have smelled to Jesus, who knew of the love in Mary's heart when she annointed His feet and wiped them with her hair.

She Showed Love

Although Mary's actions are recorded in the Bible, we know little of what she said. Mary is almost always silent. Only once do we read her words, and even then Mary repeated what Martha said after Lazarus had died. Mary fell down at Jesus' feet saying: *"Lord, if thou hadst been here, my brother had not died"* (John 11:32).

Mary gave her love silently. Often we try to show or express our love for someone with words. Sometimes we say, "I know how you are feeling," when we have not gone through a similar experience. We need to learn from Mary how powerful silent love can be. That power is made clear in Mark 14:9 when Jesus said: *"Wheresoever this gospel shall be preached throughout the whole world, this also that she hath done shall be spoken of for a memorial of her."*

Mary's act of worship motivated by love will never be forgotten. She gave all she had; she did what she could. How do we show the Lord we love Him? Do we set limits, saying we will love, serve, and give to Him only up to a certain point?

CLOSING THOUGHTS

Mary teaches us important lessons. First, we need to understand that in order to gain a deeper knowledge of God, we must spend a great deal of time in the humble position of sitting at the feet of Jesus. We must not be distracted by the activities around us or let ourselves be too busy to learn from Him.

Second, we need to do what we can to the fullest. All we have comes from God: our time, talents, money; all good gifts are from Him. We need to give ourselves to Him, holding nothing back.

Third, we need to show our love to others. Mary and Martha shared their home and what they had with others. They certainly showed their love to Jesus and the disciples. Jesus taught us to love one another. Let us do our best, with His help, to show our love to those around us.

FOR DISCUSSION

1. Describe characteristics of Mary that differ from those of Martha.
2. What did Jesus mean when He said that what Mary had chosen would not be taken away?
3. What moved Jesus to tears?
4. In what unique way did Mary express her love to Jesus?
5. What lesson you learned from Mary's life can you put into practice in your own life?

CHAPTER 45

THE SAMARITAN WOMAN

A WOMAN WITH A POWERFUL TESTIMONY

Earlier in this book we studied the harlot Rahab and Naaman's slave girl. Both of these women overcame difficult circumstances and both showed tremendous courage. In this Bible study, we will see another example of a woman who had victory over her past.

The Setting

The story about Jesus' meeting with the Samaritan woman at the well is found in John 4:1–42. Verses 4–7 supply the background:

⁴ And he must needs go through Samaria.

⁵ Then cometh he to a city of Samaria, which is called Sychar, near to the parcel of ground that Jacob gave to his son Joseph.

⁶ Now Jacob's well was there. Jesus therefore, being wearied with his journey, sat thus on the well: and it was about the sixth hour.

⁷ There cometh a woman of Samaria to draw water: Jesus saith unto her, Give me to drink.

"He must needs go through Samaria." These are strange words with which to start the Bible reading. We need to understand the background. History tells us that going through Samaria was the shortest route between Galilee and Jerusalem. The Pharisees and other Jews, however, usually took the longer route through

Peraea. Why? To avoid having any contact with the Samaritan people.

Who were the Samaritans? They were a mixed race resulting from the intermarriage of Israelites left behind when the northern kingdom was taken into exile and Gentiles who were brought into the land by the conquering Assyrians (2 Kings 17:24). Later, in Ezra chapter 4 and Nehemiah chapter 4, we read about a bitter division between the Israelites and the Samaritans which led to the construction of two temples on Mount Gerizim. They developed a deep hatred for each other, including a religious rivalry that was still strong at the time Jesus met this woman at a well.

Jesus Christ was tired and thirsty. Yet He took time to talk to the woman who came to draw water. He had never seen her before, and she obviously did not know Him. But Jesus knew she had a spiritual need. What an example for us! Do we notice the needs of others, even when we are at our best—not to mention when we are hot, thirsty, and tired? Are we willing to take time to listen to people, talk with people, and try to help meet the needs of others?

The Past Confronted

The woman was amazed that a Jewish man would talk to her and ask for a drink of water. Jews hated Samaritans, so much so that it was unusual for a Jew even to travel through Samaria. But the way Jesus spoke caught her attention. He spoke gently, but with authority, answering all her questions. Still, she misunderstood what He was saying. She was arguing defensively about the well. Jesus broke down her pride by asking her to call her husband. Immediately she was made aware of the sin in her life. She humbly acknowledged, *"I have no husband"* (John 4:17). With this honest confession, her life began to change.

Then Jesus told her about her sinful past. The woman realized Jesus must be a prophet and she changed the subject. Her concern turned to the proper place of worship. Once again Jesus corrected her, saying that the *place* of worship is not the important thing. It is the spirit of worship that counts.

The Relationship Matters

Jesus took time to explain that worship acceptable to God is found in a personal acceptance of Messiah. Finally, the woman stopped talking and listened to Jesus' teaching. The account continues in John 4:25–26:

> [25] The woman saith unto him, I know that Messiah cometh, which is called Christ: when he is come, he will tell us all things.
>
> [26] Jesus saith unto her, I that speak unto thee am he.

The woman had a bad reputation because of her immoral life. But because she freely confessed her sin, she had the privilege of hearing from Jesus' own lips the truth that He was indeed the Messiah. Jesus took time to meet her need. Her past was forgiven, and her life completely changed. In fact, when she went back to the village, the people came out to the well to hear Jesus for themselves. The Bible tells us Jesus stayed there for two days and many became believers.

CLOSING THOUGHTS

Have you ever personally accepted Jesus Christ into your life as your Savior? Is your life committed to Him? Have you ever shared with anyone what He has done in your life? The story of the woman at the well stands as an example of Jesus' personal concern for each of us. He still cares; He cares for you. He can heal your deepest hurts, calm your worst fears, and understand your innermost thoughts. He longs to bring complete change into your life through total forgiveness and cleansing.

John 4:39 says: *"And many of the Samaritans of that city believed on him for the saying of the woman, which testified, He told me all that I ever did."*

The story not only shows Jesus' love for people, but this verse gives believers in Christ an example to follow.

The Samaritan woman repented of her sin and believed Jesus, then she told others what she had seen, heard, and done. That is what Jesus wants us to do today. That is what missions is all about: telling another person who Jesus is and what He has done for you.

Think for a moment. Is there a racial group or class of people who are hated in your community? Are there people whom you and your family consider as enemies? Have you ever reached out to help them and tell them of God's love? If you don't, who will?

FOR DISCUSSION

1. Whom have you told personally what Jesus has done in your life?
2. If you were talking to Jesus today, what part of your life—past or present—would He need to discuss with you and forgive?
3. What example did Jesus give us for witnessing to others?
4. Name two ways Jesus corrected the Samaritan woman's beliefs.
5. Explain why and how the Good News of Jesus Christ crosses all barriers.

CHAPTER 46

A WOMAN
TAKEN IN ADULTERY

AN UNUSUAL MEETING WITH JESUS

Many unnamed women in the Bible can teach us lessons through their lives. In this chapter we will look at a woman who was caught in adultery, but whom Jesus saved from being stoned to death.

The Setting

Not only is this woman's name not given, we also do not know any details concerning her family or history. We know she met Jesus Christ personally and experienced His forgiveness and kindness. She saw His wisdom in action and heard Him speak.

Just before Jesus met this woman, He had spent time alone on the Mount of Olives. We are not told why Jesus was there, but we know He talked with His heavenly Father. From the Mount, He went to the temple area.

Many people came to the temple to see and hear Jesus. While He was teaching, religious leaders brought a woman to Him. They sat her down in the middle of the temple courtyard, in full view of everyone. Then they accused her of adultery and said they had caught her in the act. They reminded Jesus that the Law of Moses said she should be stoned. John 8:2–9 says:

> [2] And early in the morning he came again into the temple, and all the people came unto him; and he sat down, and taught them.

³ And the scribes and Pharisees brought unto him a woman taken in adultery; and when they had set her in the midst,

⁴ They say unto him, Master, this woman was taken in adultery, in the very act.

⁵ Now Moses in the law commanded us, that such should be stoned: but what sayest thou?

⁶ This they said, tempting him, that they might have to accuse him. But Jesus stooped down, and with his finger wrote on the ground, as though he heard them not.

⁷ So when they continued asking him, he lifted up himself, and said unto them, He that is without sin among you, let him first cast a stone at her.

⁸ And again he stooped down, and wrote on the ground.

⁹ And they which heard it, being convicted by their own conscience, went out one by one, beginning at the eldest, even unto the last: and Jesus was left alone, and the woman standing in the midst.

The Adulterer and Adulteress

This is a short story from God's Word, yet it has many lessons to teach us. First, we need to learn from the religious leaders. (They were eager to find sin in someone else's life, but were not so quick to admit their own.)They quoted the Law of Moses to Jesus as if He did not know it! But they left out one important part. They said nothing about the penalty for the man with whom she was caught committing adultery. Leviticus 20:10 states the Law: *"And the man that committeth adultery with another man's wife, even he that committeth adultery with his neighbour's wife, the adulterer and the adulteress shall surely be put to death."*

God clearly says that both the adulterer and the adulteress should be put to death! Where was the man? We will never know, because God's Word does not tell us. We need to be careful not to become proud when accusing others of sin in their lives. If only we could learn to be as quick to judge our own sin by confession to God as we are to judge the sin of others. Thank God that He has provided complete cleansing through Jesus Christ and the blood He shed on the Cross.

Forgiveness, Not Approval

It is important to realize that Jesus did not approve of what this woman did. She was guilty of adultery. Adultery is a willful violation of God's command in Exodus 20:14: *"Thou shalt not commit adultery."* In the Garden of Eden, God established and ordained marriage as a physical and spiritual union of one man and one woman for life. Genesis 2:20–24 gives clear teaching about marriage. Adultery violates that sacred union.

Jesus wisely handled the attempt of the religious leaders to trick Him. The Lord Jesus was well aware of the Law. But if He said to stone her, He would not have shown the forgiveness of sin about which He was teaching. If Jesus had said to let her go, He would have contradicted God's Law.

The woman was guilty and well aware of her sin. Even worse, everyone in the temple knew her sin. How did Jesus respond? He was silent for a while. Then looking down at the ground, He wrote in the dust.

The religious leaders were angry because Jesus did not answer their accusations. They persisted in asking Him what was to be done. The Scripture says they were "testing Him." What He said must have surprised everyone who heard Him. John 8:7 says, *"So when they continued asking him, he lifted up himself, and said unto them, He that is without sin among you, let him first cast a stone at her."*

Jesus knelt down a second time and wrote in the dust. What He wrote is open to speculation, but the result is clear. Her accusers stopped their tirade and did not throw any stones. They sheepishly retreated under the conviction of their own sinful deeds. No one can stand before God and say he has not sinned. That is why Christ's payment for our sins was necessary.

The Woman's Reaction

Did you notice that the woman remained silent? She did not try to defend herself or to blame the man. Nor did she beg for mercy. When her accusers left the temple, she could have tried to leave too. But she stayed right there and patiently waited to see what Jesus would say to her. She knew who Jesus was because she addressed Him as "Lord." John 8:10–11 concludes the account:

> [10] When Jesus had lifted up himself, and saw none but the woman, he said unto her, Woman, where are those thine accusers? Hath no man condemned thee?
> [11] She said, No man, Lord. And Jesus said unto her, Neither do I condemn thee: go, and sin no more.

Jesus gave her hope when He said, *"Neither do I condemn thee."* But at the same time He also said, *"Go, and sin no more."* Forgiveness of sin is a gift of God. But God expects men and women to do their part: stay away from sin and situations that lure you into sin. God will forgive, but how much better it is not to sin in the first place.

The Bible does not tell us any more about this woman. She probably left the temple courtyard immediately and began a new way of life.

CLOSING THOUGHTS

We can learn three scriptural lessons from this incident.

- We should be slow to point out sin in other people's lives, especially when we have not dealt with our own sin. Matthew 7:1 says, *"Judge not, that ye be not judged."*
- We need to learn to forgive others. Mark 11:25 commands, *"Forgive, if ye have ought against any: that your Father also which is in heaven may forgive you your trespasses."*

- We must learn to face the sin in our lives and to ask Jesus for forgiveness. 1 John 1:9 promises: *"If we confess our sins, he is faithful and just to forgive us our sins, and to cleanse us from all unrighteousness."*

FOR DISCUSSION

1. What does Scripture tell us about this woman's background?
2. Why is it dangerous to accuse others of sin?
3. In what way did Jesus show wisdom and compassion?
4. Explain the difference between condemning a sin and approving it.
5. Name at least three lessons you can learn from this story.

CHAPTER 47

MARY MAGDALENE

UNDERSTOOD TRUE FORGIVENESS

Like Rahab, the harlot, and the Samaritan woman, Mary Magdalene had an ugly past. Yet her story is a beautiful example of love and forgiveness.

Mary Magdalene's History

Mary was a common Jewish name. Magdala identified her birthplace. Just as Jesus was called a Nazarene because he came from Nazareth, Mary was called a Magdalene. The Bible gives no record of her parents, age, or marital status. Before meeting Jesus, she was demon possessed.

Demonic activity can be described by using three levels of satanic influence: oppression, obsession, and possession.

Oppression is an unusual pressure put on from the outside, often affecting a person's health or ability to think or function clearly. This may be seen in abnormal fears, anxieties, or some form of depression.

Obsession is a deeper or more severe oppression.

Possession, or the term "demon possessed," means a person is controlled completely by a demon or has an actual inhabitation of demons in the body. True believers in Christ cannot be possessed by demons.

Many schools of thought exist as to how much power and influence Satan and his demons can have on Christians. Satan, the father of lies and deceit, has cleverly confused and divided the Church on these teachings. However, the Bible nowhere commands Christians to cast demons out of themselves or other Christians. On the other hand, Christians are instructed to be constantly on the alert for satanic attacks and to resist them. 1 Peter 5: 8–9 instructs: *"Be sober, be vigilant; because your adversary the devil, as a roaring lion, walketh about, seeking whom he may devour; whom resist stedfast in the faith."*

Ephesians 6:10–20 gives the procedure by which believers can resist the devil by putting on the full armor of God.

Those who are demon possessed are bound by a power greater than their own. Mary Magdalene was in bondage to the demons. That does not mean, however, that she was immoral. She may have been a good person apart from the demons which lived in her.

Knowing that Mary was freed from not just one demon, but from seven, explains the extent of her devotion to Christ. We can only imagine the change that came into her life after the demonic power was broken.

After being released from the demons, Mary Magdalene was one of the most faithful of Jesus' followers. She is mentioned 14 times in the Gospels, quite often in connection with other women. Five times she is mentioned alone in connection with the death and resurrection of Jesus Christ. One of the most well-known scenes is when Jesus talked with Mary Magdalene in the garden on the morning of His resurrection.

Mary Magdalene's Faithfulness

Mary Magdalene was at the side of Mary, the mother of Jesus, on the day of the crucifixion. She experienced great sorrow. On Resurrection morning, she was among the first at the garden tomb. Imagine how she must have felt when she saw the empty tomb. With tears in her eyes, she ran to tell Peter and John. Together they returned to the tomb. When Peter and John saw the empty tomb for themselves, they returned home, but Mary did not. She stood near the empty tomb, weeping, as we read in John 20:11–17:

[11] But Mary stood without at the sepulchre weeping: and as she wept, she stooped down, and looked into the sepulchre,

[12] And seeth two angels in white sitting, the one at the head, and the other at the feet, where the body of Jesus had lain.

[13] And they say unto her, Woman, why weepest thou? She saith unto them, Because they have taken away my Lord, and I know not where they have laid him.

[14] And when she had thus said, she turned herself back, and saw Jesus standing, and knew not that it was Jesus.

[15] Jesus saith unto her, Woman, why weepest thou? whom seekest thou? She, supposing him to be the gardener, saith unto him, Sir, if thou have borne him hence, tell me where thou hast laid him, and I will take him away.

[16] Jesus saith unto her, Mary. She turned herself, and saith unto him, Rabboni; which is to say, Master.

[17] Jesus saith unto her, Touch me not; for I am not yet ascended to my Father: but go to my brethren, and say unto them, I ascend unto my Father, and your Father; and to my God, and your God.

Jesus gave Mary Magdalene an honor which will never be taken away. She was the first person to see the risen Savior and the first to hear Him speak after His resurrection. When she recognized His voice, her first reaction was to touch Him. Jesus would not permit her to do so. Maybe she needed to understand that His human presence was no longer necessary in her life. She needed to learn about a closer, spiritual communion with God. This was a totally new concept and would be a new relationship that would last after the Lord Jesus went back to heaven.

CLOSING THOUGHTS

Mary Magdalene could have sunk into total despair because of her past life or her present circumstances. She could have blamed God. She could have been bitter or suffered from a sense of guilt and shame. Rather, she rose above her past to serve God.

You can do the same today through a personal relationship with Jesus Christ. John 8:36 says, *"If the Son therefore shall make you free, ye shall be free indeed."* You may find yourself in bondage to fear, drugs or alcohol, pornography, or myriad other controlling influences. Come to the Lord Jesus Christ in repentance and faith. He will set you free.

FOR DISCUSSION

1. What instructions are given to believers in Jesus Christ in relation to Satan?
2. How was Mary's life changed after Jesus released her from demonic bondage?
3. Why was Mary so devoted to Jesus?
4. What is your motive for serving God?
5. Are you—or is anyone you know—in bondage to any substance or influence? What promise is given in John 8:36? Explain how forgiveness gives freedom in a person's life.

CHAPTER 48

SAPPHIRA

A DECEITFUL WOMAN

I pray this lesson will be a solemn reminder to each of us of the seriousness of sin. We will study the sins of deceit and lying, which the Bible calls "an abomination in God's eyes" in Proverbs 12:22.

Soon after Jesus returned to heaven, the early Christians formed the first church in Jerusalem. With the help of the Holy Spirit, the church grew daily. In that early church were a husband and wife whose names were Ananias and Sapphira.

Background

The Bible doesn't give us any information about Ananias and Sapphira's history, family, or wealth. All we know is that they jointly agreed to lie about their money. To put the situation in proper context, we need to read Acts 4:32, 34–35:

> [32] And the multitude of them that believed were of one heart and of one soul: neither said any of them that ought of the things which he possessed was his own; but they had all things common.
>
> [34] Neither was there any among them that lacked: for as many as were possessors of lands or houses sold them, and brought the prices of the things that were sold,
>
> [35] And laid them down at the apostles' feet: and distribution was made unto every man according as he had need.

Notice these early Christians in Jerusalem agreed to share what they had with one another. They also agreed to establish a common fund for distribution to the needy. No one forced this on members of the group; participation was completely voluntary. That is important to keep in mind.

Their Evil Agreement

With that background, we begin the story of Ananias and Sapphira as found in Acts 5:1–4. At the end of Acts 4, we find the account of Barnabas, who sold his land and gave the money to the apostles. By way of contrast, chapter 5 begins with the word *"But."*

> ¹ But a certain man named Ananias, with Sapphira his wife, sold a possession,
>
> ² And kept back part of the price, his wife also being privy to it, and brought a certain part, and laid it at the apostles' feet.
>
> ³ But Peter said, Ananias, why hath Satan filled thine heart to lie to the Holy Ghost, and to keep back part of the price of the land?
>
> ⁴ Whiles it remained, was it not thine own? and after it was sold, was it not in thine own power? why hast thou conceived this thing in thine heart? thou hast not lied unto men, but unto God.

Their Sin

Like Barnabas, Ananias and Sapphira also sold a piece of land, but they agreed together to keep part of the money for themselves. Some people accuse them of being greedy, but the Bible points out a different sin—deceit. Keeping back some of their own money was not a sin. It was theirs to keep or give away in whole or in part. They sinned because they tried to give the impression to others in the church that they were giving *all* the money they received from the sale.

Their scheme was a definite act of deceit. That is why Peter sternly rebuked them for lying to the Holy Spirit. The consequences are clearly stated in Acts 5:5–6:

> [5] And as he heard these words, Ananias fell down and breathed his last; and great fear came upon all who heard of it.
>
> [6] And the young men arose and covered him up, and after carrying him out, they buried him.

About three hours later, Sapphira came to the assembly of believers. The apostle Peter confronted her about the money. Sapphira lied, and she, too, dropped dead. Acts 5:7–10 states:

> [7] And it was about the space of three hours after, when his wife, not knowing what was done, came in.
>
> [8] And Peter answered unto her, Tell me whether ye sold the land for so much? And she said, Yea, for so much.
>
> [9] Then Peter said unto her, How is it that ye have agreed together to tempt the Spirit of the Lord? behold, the feet of them which have buried thy husband are at the door, and shall carry thee out.
>
> [10] Then fell she down straightway at his feet, and yielded up the ghost: and the young men came in, and found her dead, and, carrying her forth, buried her by her husband.

The Result of Their Deceit

Sapphira made a clear choice to go along with her husband in his dishonesty. Her loyalty was to her husband rather than to God. When Peter asked her the direct question about the money, she lied, apparently without shame.

Ananias and Sapphira both died because of one lie. This is hard for us to understand. But I believe God's purpose in doing this was that what happened to them might be an eternal testimony to how terrible lying is in God's sight. The church in Jerusalem was the first church. They had many lessons to learn, and the Bible says great fear came on everyone who heard what had happened. No one had any doubt as to how God felt about lying.

CLOSING THOUGHTS

What about us today? Do we think the sin of lying is any less severe in God's eyes today than it was in Bible times? It is not. We need to examine our lives to see whether or not we are honest at all times. There is no middle ground on any given issue when we are confronted. Either we speak the truth or we don't. If what we say is not the truth, then it is a lie.

We must realize that those who live with us know how honest we really are. As a mother, have you ever let the kids do something their dad had said no to, such as watching a certain movie or going to a particular place? And then, after the episode, saying to them, "Don't tell Daddy; this will be our little secret!"

Do you spend more money than you can afford on clothing, cosmetics, furniture, or jewelry so you'll look richer than you are?

How do you talk when no one is around but you and the kids? Do you yell or even swear on the way to church, but then talk sweetly to the pastor and others when you get there?

These are subtle ways we show our children and those around us that lying and being deceitful is acceptable. Are we setting examples that teach our children to tell the truth? Or do they see us trying to deceitfully arrange things so that we will look good when others see us.

Let's ask God to forgive us and to help us live honest lives. Meditate on the following verses to see what God says about lying:

- *"Lying lips are abomination to the LORD: but they that deal truly are his delight"* (Proverbs 12:22).

- *"Deliver my soul, O LORD, from lying lips, and from a deceitful tongue"* (Psalm 120:2).
- *"Wherefore putting away lying, speak every man truth with his neighbour"* (Ephesians 4:25)

FOR DISCUSSION

1. Explain how members in the early Church helped one another.
2. On what specific issue did Sapphira agree with her husband?
3. Did she and her husband sin in keeping some of their money for themselves?
4. Why do you think God punished this matter so severely and so quickly?
5. Discuss the seriousness of lying. How can we teach this to children?

CHAPTER 49

DORCAS

A GENEROUS HELPER

Someone once said, "It is amazing how much can be accomplished when no one cares who gets the credit." This was true of Dorcas, who did her duty without considering how far the consequences of her work might go.

The Bible uses just seven verses to tell about Dorcas' life. Yet she is an example to women everywhere of the importance of helping others—and how doing this reflects on our Christian testimony.

Background

Dorcas lived in a seaport called Joppa. She lived during the time of the formation of the early Church shortly after Jesus' resurrection. The Church was growing steadily and rapidly under the apostle Peter's leadership.

The Bible calls Dorcas a "disciple," which means follower of Christ. We are not told where she learned of Him, where she learned to sew, or why she was so concerned for the widows.

Her story is found in Acts 9:36–42. Verse 36 begins, *"Now there was at Joppa a certain disciple named Tabitha, which by interpretation is called Dorcas: this woman was full of good works and almsdeeds which she did."*

Tabitha is the Hebrew equivalent of the Greek name Dorcas. In Greek, Dorcas means "gazelle," an emblem of beauty. We don't know if Dorcas was a beautiful woman or not, but she showed the beauty of Jesus in her life by the compassion she demonstrated to people in need.

Dorcas: "Full of Good Works"

The phrase "full of good works" indicates she actually performed good deeds. She didn't just think about doing something to help people. Often, we have good intentions, but never quite get around to doing anything. Or we become overwhelmed by all the needs around us. We know we cannot meet everyone's needs, so we don't even try to help the one or two people we could help.

Dorcas was not like that. She did what she could. Our testimonies for Christ would be much more effective if we just did what we intend to do! We need to ask God to help us to be quick, willing, and ready to follow the prompting of the Holy Spirit in doing good works. Let us be quite clear about this matter. We do not receive salvation by doing good works. Salvation is a free gift from God which we receive through faith in Jesus Christ. In explaining salvation, we often quote Ephesians 2:8–9: *"For by grace are ye saved through faith; and that not of yourselves: it is the gift of God: not of works, lest any man should boast."*

We are not saved by doing good works, but we show that we have received salvation when we do good works. Ephesians 2:10 continues the thought: *"For we are his workmanship, created in Christ Jesus **unto good works**, which God hath before ordained that we should walk in them."*

James 2:14–17 explains the influence our works can have on others. In fact, God tells us that our faith is dead if we do not demonstrate our good works. Dorcas was a good example of James' teaching: *"What doth it profit, my brethren, though a man say he hath faith, and have not works? can faith save him? If a brother or sister be naked, and destitute of daily food. And one of you say unto them, Depart in peace, be ye warmed and filled; notwithstanding ye give them not those things which are needful to the body; what doth it prof-it? Even so faith, if it hath not works, is dead, being alone."*

Dorcas: Sick Unto Death

We read in Acts 9:37–42 that Dorcas became sick and died.

³⁷ And it came to pass in those days, that she was sick, and died: whom when they had washed, they laid her in an upper chamber.

³⁸ And forasmuch as Lydda was nigh to Joppa, and the disciples had heard that Peter was there, they sent unto him two men, desiring him that he would not delay to come to them.

³⁹ Then Peter arose and went with them. When he was come, they brought him into the upper chamber: and all the widows stood by him weeping, and shewing the coats and garments which Dorcas made, while she was with them.

⁴⁰ But Peter put them all forth, and kneeled down, and prayed; and turning him to the body said, Tabitha, arise. And she opened her eyes: and when she saw Peter, she sat up.

⁴¹ And he gave her his hand, and lifted her up, and when he had called the saints and widows, presented her alive.

⁴² And it was known throughout all Joppa; and many believed in the Lord.

What a sight when Peter arrived in the room where Dorcas lay! We don't know if Dorcas had family of her own. But when she died, those she had helped took care of her body. They also sent two men to ask Peter to come. Dorcas obviously meant much to these people. Her love and service as a seamstress endeared her to them.

What did these believers expect from Peter? The Bible doesn't say, but they did expect something. Comfort in their sorrow is one thing they wanted. Perhaps they also wanted guidance about what to do next. Maybe they hoped Peter could perform a miracle. Through God's power, he had done other miracles. Whatever they expected, the fact that they sent for a man of God shows their respect and belief in the God whom Dorcas trusted.

Dorcas: Revived by God

Peter arrived and evaluated the situation. He sent everyone out of the room so he could be alone with God. We do not know what he prayed or what he asked God to do. But God performed a miracle and restored Dorcas to life.

After Dorcas opened her eyes and got up, Peter presented her to the people who had been mourning her death. Quickly the scene changed as their tears turned to shouts of joy.

The people closest to Dorcas were greatly blessed by what God had done for her. But the blessing did not stop there. Acts 42 tells us that the miracle was known all around, and many believed in the Lord. The early Church grew in number, but more importantly, I am sure their faith in God and His power also greatly increased.

CLOSING THOUGHTS

I am glad God included the life of Dorcas in His Word. She was described as being full of good works. She helped needy people who might otherwise have been forgotten.

Dorcas' activities remind us of Jesus' words in Matthew 25:40: *"Verily I say unto you, Inasmuch as ye have done it unto one of the least of these my brethren, ye have done it unto me."*

Can you think of someone who needs your help today? We may not all be able to sew like Dorcas. Some might be able to cook a meal for a needy family, help clean a house, offer to care for children so a mother can get some rest, tutor students, teach music, visit someone in the hospital, or read to a blind person. The list of ways we can be of help to others is endless, limited only by our imagination. Ask God to show you what you can do and then—like Dorcas—do it.

FOR DISCUSSION

1. Why do you think God included this story in the Bible?
2. Name three lessons you can learn from the life of Dorcas.
3. Describe the miracle God performed in Dorcas' life. Why do you think God gave her life back?
4. List five people whom you could help. What can you do to help them? What is your plan to *do* this?
5. Why is doing good for those around us important?

CHAPTER 50

RHODA

A PERSISTENT MAID

In His Word, God tells about the lives of women we would think of as being great, but He also tells about those whom we would call insignificant. This chapter is about a young servant girl named Rhoda. She worked in the home of Mary, the mother of John Mark, who wrote the gospel of Mark. The name Rhoda means "rose." Rhoda's story starts when she answered a knock at the door during the night.

Background

During this time of Church history, Christians were being persecuted. Mary apparently had a large home where Christians in Jerusalem often met to worship and pray. On this particular night, they were praying earnestly for Peter, who was in prison. There was a strong possibility Peter would be killed the next day because King Herod already had ordered the execution of the apostle James.

While the Christians were praying, the Lord sent an angel who helped Peter escape from prison. When Peter found himself on the streets of Jerusalem, he went directly to Mary's home and knocked on the door. Rhoda came to the door. She recognized Peter's voice, but got so excited she forgot to open the door and let him in. Acts 12:3–16 gives the account:

> ³ And because he [King Herod] saw it pleased the Jews, he proceeded further to take Peter also. (Then were the days of unleavened bread.)

⁴ And when he had apprehended him, he put him in prison, and delivered him to four quaternions of soldiers to keep him; intending after Easter to bring him forth to the people.

⁵ Peter therefore was kept in prison: but prayer was made without ceasing of the church unto God for him.

⁶ And when Herod would have brought him forth, the same night Peter was sleeping between two soldiers, bound with two chains: and the keepers before the door kept the prison.

⁷ And, behold, the angel of the Lord came upon him, and a light shined in the prison: and he smote Peter on the side, and raised him up, saying, Arise up quickly. And his chains fell off from his hands.

⁸ And the angel said unto him, Gird thyself, and bind on thy sandals. And so he did. And he saith unto him, Cast thy garment about thee, and follow me.

⁹ And he went out, and followed him; and wist not that it was true which was done by the angel; but thought he saw a vision.

¹⁰ When they were past the first and the second ward, they came unto the iron gate that leadeth unto the city; which opened to them of his own accord: and they went out, and passed on through one street; and forthwith the angel departed from him.

¹¹ And when Peter was come to himself, he said, Now I know of a surety, that the Lord hath sent his angel, and hath delivered me out of the hand of Herod, and from all the expectation of the people of the Jews.

¹² And when he had considered the thing, he came to the house of Mary the mother of John, whose surname was Mark; where many were gathered together praying.

¹³ And as Peter knocked at the door of the gate, a damsel came to hearken, named Rhoda.

¹⁴ And when she knew Peter's voice, she opened not the gate for gladness, but ran in, and told how Peter stood before the gate.

¹⁵ And they said unto her, Thou art mad. But she constantly affirmed that it was even so. Then said they, It is his angel.

¹⁶ But Peter continued knocking: and when they had opened the door, and saw him, they were astonished.

God's Part and Our Part

God performed a miracle by getting Peter out of prison. However, He did not miraculously open the door at Mary's house to let Peter in. This illustrates the principle called the "divine/human co-operative," which means God often helps people when there is nothing they can do to help themselves. But some things God expects human beings to do for themselves. In this situation, people inside the house were perfectly able to open the door, so God did not do that for them.

Fear and unbelief caused the delay in opening the door for Peter. It could have been a dangerous situation if soldiers on patrol had recognized Peter. He and the other Christians gathered in the house could have been arrested. Notice that it was not Rhoda's unbelief that caused the delay in opening the door to Peter. Rhoda recognized that God had answered prayer and ran to tell the others. The problem was that the older people refused to believe a young servant girl's words.

Rhoda displayed two characteristics we need in our lives: joy and persistence.

Joy in Answered Prayer

Joy and happiness encompassed her when she knew God had answered their prayers. Rhoda recognized Peter's voice, so we know he must have spoken to her as well as knocked on the door. Rhoda was so happy and excited that she interrupted the prayer meeting to tell the people their answer stood at the door.

Why was she so happy? In order for the answer to prayer to have brought such joy into her life, she, too, must have been a believer and prayed for Peter's deliverance.

Persistence

In spite of the fact that she was just a servant, Rhoda ignored the others mocking her and insisted that Peter was at the door. It was the others who did not believe God could answer their prayers so soon!

When they heard Rhoda's words, the other Christians accused her of being "out of her mind." Then they said she must be seeing "his angel." But Rhoda insisted that Peter, indeed, was standing at the door. It was only when they heard Peter's continued knocking that they went to open the door and let him into the house.

CLOSING THOUGHTS

Sometimes when we face strong opposition, it seems easier just to give in, even if we know the truth. But that is the time to stand firm. It is also easy for us to be surprised when God answers our prayers. We need to be thankful we have a patient heavenly Father who still loves us and answers our prayers, sometimes in spite of our unbelief.

Rhoda's joy in the Lord and strength of character to stand up for the truth were of value to the early Church. These same attributes are valuable today and need to be part of our lives.

Let us appreciate good characteristics in other Christians, even if they are of a different social standing. Rhoda was only a servant girl who waited on others. However, she was the first to hear Peter's voice and to spread the news that God had answered their prayers.

God still answers prayer today! The next time He answers prayer for you, don't be surprised. Remember to thank Him. Jesus gives this promise in 1 John 5:14–15: *"If we ask anything according to his will*, he heareth us: *And if we know that he hear us, whatsoever we ask, we know that we have the petitions that we desired of him."*

FOR DISCUSSION
1. What information does the Bible give about Rhoda?
2. Why was Peter knocking at the door?
3. Explain the principle of God doing His part while man does what he can.
4. Why was Rhoda such a help to the early Church?
5. How do you react when God answers your prayer?

CHAPTER 51

LYDIA

A BUSINESSWOMAN WHO SERVED

In this chapter we will discuss a woman named Lydia. She was known for two things: being a successful businesswoman, and showing her hospitality.

Background

Lydia was a Gentile from the city of Thyatira in the western part of Asia Minor, which is known today as Turkey. Thyatira was a business center at that time. Lydia had her own business, selling purple fabric, a color that was expensive because of the dyeing process. Most likely, Lydia was wealthy, successful, and influential. The apostle Paul, Silas, and Luke, the author of Acts, were traveling together when they reached the city of Philippi, where they met Lydia. Although Lydia originally came from Thyatira, at the time of her encounter with Paul she had a home in Philippi (on the European continent). We read her story in Acts 16:13–15:

> [13] And on the sabbath we went out of the city by a river side, where prayer was wont to be made; and we sat down, and spake unto the women which resorted thither.
> [14] And a certain woman named Lydia, a seller of purple, of the city of Thyatira, which worshipped God, heard us: whose heart the Lord opened, that she attended unto the things which were spoken of Paul.

¹⁵ And when she was baptized, and her household, she besought us, saying, If ye have judged me to be faithful to the Lord, come into my house, and abide there. And she constrained us.

Why does God include Lydia in the Bible? Why should she be an example to us? We know very little about her background or family connections. At the time she met Paul, she was a prosperous businesswoman.

Lydia's Open Heart

There is another side to her, however. Lydia was a person with a heart open to God. Acts 16:14 says it is the Lord who opened her heart. We know God does not force Himself upon anyone, so Lydia must have been willing to allow God to work in her life. Her open heart caused her not only to hear what Paul said, but also to respond by accepting the Good News about Jesus Christ.

Where was Lydia when "The Lord opened her heart"? It was the Sabbath day, the day of worship for the Jews, and Lydia was at the place where women gathered to pray. She was in the right place at the right time. Maybe some of us miss hearing God speak to us because we are not present at church services, Bible studies, and prayer meetings. Hebrews 10:25 advises believers not to forsake assembling together.

Acts 16:14 also says Lydia was "a worshiper of God." Lydia looked for truth because she longed to worship God. In Jeremiah 29:13 we read this promise: *"And ye shall seek me, and find me, when ye search for me with all your heart."* Lydia sought after God, and God led Paul to the very spot where the women were praying.

Lydia had to take time away from her business in order to pray. Today, too, it takes time to listen to God. Are you willing to give that time? Maybe you have a successful business that occupies most of your time. Or maybe you are struggling to make a living and have little time to worship God. Maybe your studies, family responsibilities, or a thousand other activities fill up your day. Like Lydia, you and I must take time to hear what God is saying.

Lydia's Testimony

After Lydia believed, she immediately gave public testimony to her faith in Jesus Christ. She and her entire household were baptized (Acts 16:15). The apostle Paul discusses the meaning of baptism in Romans 6:4–5: *"Therefore we are buried with him by baptism into death: that like as Christ was raised up from the dead by the glory of the Father, even so we also should walk in newness of life. For if we have been planted together in the likeness of his death, we shall be also in the likeness of his resurrection."*

Baptism does not save a person from eternal damnation. It is an outward sign of a believer's inner relationship with Jesus Christ. Baptism is a picture: a believer is placed under the water to show the death and burial of Christ and raised up from the water to show Christ's resurrection from the dead.

Many times throughout the book of Acts we read the words So-and-so *"believed and was baptized."* The early Christians, like Lydia, set the example. If you have believed in Jesus as your personal Savior, you should be baptized. In doing so, you publicly demonstrate your obedience to our Lord's command and, to all who witness it, your desire to live for Jesus.

Lydia showed great enthusiasm in her belief and service for the Lord. What is our reaction when God has satisfied our deepest longings and answered our prayers, whether big or small? Some of us keep these joys to ourselves. Are we hesitant to share what God has done in our lives, especially with those closest to us? Jesus spoke strong words of warning on this subject in Matthew 10:32–33: *"Whosoever therefore shall confess me before men, him will I confess also before my Father which is in heaven. But whosoever shall deny me before men, him will I also deny before my Father which is in heaven."*

The Lord blessed Lydia's open witness. She is considered to be the first convert of the apostle Paul's missionary work in Europe. And God let it be a woman!

Lydia's Open Home

Acts 16:15 tells us that Lydia urged Paul and his companions to stay with her. Chapter 16 continues by telling what happened to Paul and Silas while they were in Philippi. In Acts 16:23, we learn that they were stripped and beaten, then thrown into prison. The jailer was commanded to guard them carefully. So he put them in the inner cell and fastened their feet in chains. During the night Paul and Silas prayed and sang hymns. Because of their testimony, the jailer asked Paul, *"What must I do to be saved?"* (Acts 16:30). Paul's answer in Acts 16:31 is the clearest explanation of how a person receives salvation: *"Believe on the Lord Jesus Christ, and thou shalt be saved, and thy house."*

When Paul and Silas were released from prison, they returned to Lydia's house. She once again opened her home and cared for them. Lydia was not ashamed to have these godly men in her home even though they had just been released from prison.

Lydia did not stop her work when she became a Christian. She probably knew many business people and traders from other parts of the world. But Paul and Silas were more important to her than business. She did not shrink from helping them just because having them around might hurt business. God will see that our needs are met when we put Him first in our lives. Matthew 6:33 gives this teaching: *"Seek ye first the kingdom of God, and his righteousness; and all these things shall be added unto you."*

Philippians 4:19 promises, *"My God shall supply all your needs according to his riches in glory by Christ Jesus."*

CLOSING THOUGHTS

The apostle Paul is very much a part of Lydia's story. He was sensitive to the leading of the Holy Spirit and was obedient to God. He went to the place of worship and spoke to the women there. Lives were changed because of Paul's teaching.

We need to ask ourselves, "Am I sensitive to the Holy Spirit? Am I obedient to God's leading in my life? Do I know His Word well enough to recognize His leading?" In Ephesians 5:17 Paul says, "Wherefore be ye not unwise, but understanding what the will of the Lord is."

The only way to understand God's will is to read and meditate on His Word.

Perhaps you sense God telling you to do something. Check it against the written Word of God. God will never lead you to do something contrary to His Word. When it is clear what God wants you to do, follow Paul's example. Do not be afraid or ashamed to do what God is telling you. You never know when there might be someone—perhaps a Lydia—listening with an open heart.

FOR DISCUSSION

1. What two things was Lydia known for?
2. Where was Lydia when she first met the apostle Paul? Why is this significant?
3. Explain the importance of baptism.
4. In what ways did Lydia help Paul and Silas?
5. Can you think of a time in your life when you were seeking God and He made Himself known to you? Can you think of a time when God supplied your need? Have you shared this testimony with others?

CHAPTER 52

PRISCILLA

UNITED IN MINISTRY WITH HER HUSBAND

Most of us have admired or respected someone who influenced us because of a godly life. Aquila and Priscilla probably felt that way about the apostle Paul, with whom they worked in tentmaking and in evangelism. In this chapter we will study their lives.

Aquila and Priscilla are always mentioned together in the Bible. It is not possible for every husband and wife to work together the way this couple did. However, even if their jobs physically separate them during working hours, couples can still be united in spirit. We will see this in the story of Aquila and Priscilla as told in Acts 18:1–3:

¹ After these things Paul departed from Athens, and came to Corinth;

² And found a certain Jew named Aquila, born in Pontus, lately come from Italy, with his wife Priscilla; (because that Claudius had commanded all Jews to depart from Rome:) and came unto them.

³ And because he was of the same craft, he abode with them, and wrought: for by their occupation they were tentmakers.

The Bible does not tell us when or how Aquila and Priscilla came to know the Lord. They may have known the Lord already when Paul came to visit, or Paul may have led them to accept

Jesus Christ as their Savior. But they were united in their love for each other, as well as for the Lord they served.

God worked through Aquila and Priscilla to provide fellowship for Paul. But they provided more than just companionship; they also provided physically for Paul by letting him stay in their home.

Their Occupation

From the previous verses we learn that Aquila and Priscilla were tent-makers. Not only were they united in marriage and in their love for the Lord, they also worked in the same trade. They shared the duties of the shop and ran their business together.

Paul was a tent-maker by trade. Later in Acts 18, we read that Paul stayed with Aquila and Priscilla, at least for part of the 18 months he spent in Corinth. From other verses in the Bible, we know Paul sometimes made tents to earn money for his own daily needs. When Paul was not preaching or teaching, I am sure the trio had many conversations about their trade and their love for the Lord.

Teachers Trained by Paul

While Paul was in Aquila and Priscilla's home, we can imagine they listened to his teaching, watched his life, learned from his example, and prayed with him and for him. Aquila and Priscilla gained much from their united service and open hospitality to one of God's servants.

Continuing in Acts 18, we read that when Paul left Corinth, he took Aquila and Priscilla with him. Paul left the couple to work in Ephesus while he went on alone.

After all the training Aquila and Priscilla received from Paul, they were able to serve God by helping a man named Apollos. Acts 18:24–26 tells us:

> [24] And a certain Jew named Apollos, born at Alexandria, an eloquent man, and mighty in the scriptures, came to Ephesus.

²⁵ This man was instructed in the way of the Lord; and being fervent in the spirit, he spake and taught diligently the things of the Lord, knowing only the baptism of John.

²⁶ And he began to speak boldly in the synagogue: whom when Aquila and Priscilla had heard, they took him unto them, and expounded unto him the way of God more perfectly.

We can learn an important lesson from these verses. Aquila and Priscilla listened to Apollos before passing judgment. They knew his teaching was correct, but fell short of the full truth of the Gospel. However, they did not publicly criticize him. The Bible says they took him aside and "explained to him the way of God more accurately."

By the time Paul wrote 1 Corinthians, Apollos had become so well known he was named with the apostles Paul and Peter as one whose teaching was highly regarded. Divisions in the Corinthian church centered on specific teachers. Paul corrects the people in 1 Corinthians 3:4–8, saying that the error is with those who separate themselves from others based on the teaching of a man, whether he is Peter, Apollos, or Paul himself. It is not the teacher who is important; it is the content of his teaching that matters.

Apollos owed much to Priscilla and Aquila for explaining God's way to him. Notice how God uses people in His service. Not everyone is meant to be a Paul or an Apollos. But God may use one of us to help make someone else great. Those humble tent-makers, Aquila and Priscilla, greatly enriched the ministry of Apollos, whom God used mightily in the early churches.

We don't read much more about Aquila and Priscilla. But in Romans 16:3–5, Paul gives another look at their lives:

³ Greet Priscilla and Aquila my helpers in Christ Jesus:

⁴ Who have for my life laid down their own necks: unto whom not only I give thanks, but also all the churches of the Gentiles.

⁵ Likewise greet the church that is in their house.

Paul did not forget his friends. Paul knew Aquila and Priscilla had even risked their lives for him and for the sake of the Gospel. At that time, poverty and persecution made it almost impossible to build church buildings. So Christians met in homes. One of the risks Aquila and Priscilla took was to hold church in their home. Once again we see the couple united—this time in the use of their home.

CLOSING THOUGHTS

What have we learned from Aquila and Priscilla? The first thing is to seek recognition only from God for our service to Him. It doesn't matter if we are "big names" in the Church, but it does matter that we are faithful to do our part in helping the entire body of Christ grow stronger.

Another lesson we can learn is from their marriage. They were one in their work, their hospitality, their service, and their study of the Scriptures. This does not mean that a married woman gifted with a good business ability or other skills and professions should not use those abilities. A husband truly united with his wife will want her to do her best using the gifts God has given her. As he encourages her, prays for her, supports her, and publicly recognizes her good works, he can be in one spirit with her.

This story is about a married couple and the example they set. But it does not mean that a single parent or unmarried career woman can not have a sense of accomplishment in her work. A few words of caution apply, however, in this day when so many homes are broken and there is so much jealousy in marriages over who gets the most attention. I think married women should look closely at this Bible story. Some married women feel they must have their own work, their own recognition and sense of accomplishment apart from their husband. A true sense of accomplishment comes from doing the will of God, not in going our separate ways. I think we should take seriously the example of Priscilla, who stood side by side with her husband.

If you are married, are you one with your husband? If not, ask God to break down your pride and independent spirit. Our churches would be much stronger if all Christian marriages were as united as Priscilla and Aquila's marriage was.

FOR DISCUSSION
1. Explain three ways Priscilla was united with her husband.
2. In what two ways did Aquila and Priscilla help the apostle Paul?
3. Under what circumstance did God use them to help Apollos?
4. How did they risk their lives for the sake of the Gospel?
5. In what way is their marriage an example for today's couples?

CHAPTER 53

EUNICE

A WOMAN WHO TRAINED HER SON

The Bible teaches that training a child in the fear and admonition of the Lord is the responsibility of the parents. In this chapter, we will see a home where this responsibility was carried out remarkably well.

Background

The woman of this home was Eunice. She and her mother, Lois, are mentioned several times in the Bible, and always together. Probably they lived together.

The child in this home was Eunice's son, Timothy. As we study Timothy's home life and see the way he was reared, let us ask God to help us use our influence in a positive way in the lives of children in our circle of influence.

Eunice is a Greek name meaning "a good or happy victory." Although she had a Greek name, Eunice was a Jewess who dearly loved the Lord. Her husband was Greek. We read this in Acts 16:1–3:

> [1] Then came he to Derbe and Lystra: and, behold, a certain disciple was there, named Timotheus, the son of a certain woman, which was a Jewess, and believed; but his father was a Greek:
> [2] Which was well reported of by the brethren that were at Lystra and Iconium.

³ Him would Paul have to go forth with him; and took and circumcised him because of the Jews which were in those quarters: for they knew all that his father was a Greek.

The Bible does not tell us Eunice's husband's name. Perhaps he had died, leaving Eunice a widow by the time of this writing. If so, Eunice was a single mom rearing a son. On the other hand, it was common knowledge that Timothy's father was Greek, and nowhere do we read that he was dead. If he was alive, Eunice's was a divided home in which one parent was a believer in God and the other was not. God is faithful to help you have a Christian home, even if your spouse is not a believer.

In any case, Eunice and her mother shared the very important role of carefully and wisely rearing young Timothy.

Timothy's Upbringing

Whatever the situation in his home, it is the training Timothy received which is emphasized in Scripture. The story of Timothy (the son), Eunice (the mother), and Lois (the grandmother) is one of the strongest trios stemming from the maternal line of any family in the New Testament.

2 Timothy 1:5 gives special insight into Eunice's character. Paul writes: *"When I call to remembrance the unfeigned faith that is in thee, which dwelt first in thy grandmother Lois, and thy mother Eunice; and I am persuaded that in thee also."*

This verse reflects how well Eunice instilled into Timothy characteristics that were pleasing to God. God blessed Eunice by using her son in His work. Parents have no greater joy than seeing their children following and serving the Lord.

Timothy's Service for God

Paul calls Eunice's son "my beloved son" (2 Timothy 1:2). This is because Paul led Timothy to the Lord, then took him on missionary travels as a companion, an evangelist, and, later, as pastor in Ephesus. Because Paul took Timothy along when he was just a boy, Timothy was associated with Paul longer than any of Paul's other companions.

Eunice had prepared her son for such responsibilities. It must have been both a sad and a happy day when Timothy left to work with the apostle Paul.

Eunice reminds me of another woman, Hannah, who gave her son to God to serve in the temple of the Lord. Hannah also prepared her son for his life's work.

Eunice and Lois would have known the story of Hannah and Samuel. They might have known the words of King Solomon in Proverbs 23:24–25: *"He that begetteth a wise child shall have joy of him. Thy father and thy mother shall be glad, and she that bare thee shall rejoice."*

Paul's Tribute to Eunice and Lois

In 2 Timothy 3:10, 13–15, which he wrote near the end of his life, Paul gave an outstanding memorial to Timothy's mother and grandmother. It sheds light on their character and on the training Eunice and Lois gave Timothy:

[10] But thou hast fully known my doctrine, manner of life, purpose, faith, longsuffering, charity, patience,

[13] But evil men and seducers shall wax worse and worse, deceiving, and being deceived.

[14] But continue thou in the things which thou hast learned and hast been assured of, knowing of whom thou hast learned them;

[15] And that from a child thou hast known the holy scriptures, which are able to make thee wise unto salvation through faith which is in Christ Jesus.

CLOSING THOUGHTS

We can learn many lessons from Eunice and her example in teaching her son. One is the value of positive Christian training in the home and in the lives of our children. The book of

Proverbs gives many verses that discuss the training of children:

- *"Train up a child in the way he should go: and when he is old, he will not depart from it"* (Proverbs 22:6).
- *"My son, despise not the chastening of the LORD; neither be weary of his correction: For whom the LORD loveth he correcteth; even as a father the son in whom he delighteth"* (Proverbs 3:11–12).
- *"He that spareth his rod hateth his son: but he that loveth him chasteneth him betimes"* (Proverbs 13:24).

It takes time and effort to teach children. It also takes the special wisdom which comes only from God. Mothers and teachers need to make training children a priority, not allowing other things to get in the way.

Another truth we need to understand is that just because Eunice instilled her beliefs in Timothy, it was not her faith that gave him salvation. Timothy had to personally put his trust in Jesus Christ in order to be saved from sin. This is important. Parents need to bring children to the place where they understand their own need for salvation. After children put their trust in the Lord as their Savior, parents must help them grow in their faith and in the knowledge of the Lord Jesus.

Whoever you are—mother, grandmother, aunt, teacher—ask God to help you be the kind of example that will lead the children under your influence to God.

FOR DISCUSSION

1. List three reasons it is important to teach children Christian principles at a young age.
2. Where did Eunice learn her life principles?
3. From where or whom could a child receive godly teaching if not from his parents?
4. What two lessons does Eunice teach by her example?
5. Name three ways your home can be an example of a Christian home in your community.

CHAPTER 54

THE GODLY WOMAN

PROVERBS 31

As we conclude this study, I thought it would be good to review the first chapter—where we looked at the characteristics of the virtuous woman in Proverbs 31. Those of us who love the Lord desire to be women who will please God.

A Second Look at the Virtuous Woman

Looking at Proverbs 31:10, we find the rhetorical question *"Who can find a virtuous woman? For her price is far above rubies."* Nothing more can be added to the beauty of this biblical portrait of the godly woman. Her chastity, love, diligence, efficiency, earnestness, devotion, and business skills are all beautifully described in Proverbs 31:11–31.

Reviewing these verses will, I trust, help us examine our own lives. With God's help, we can correct areas in our lives that need attention.

She Serves Her Family Well

Proverbs 31:11–31 tells us about the godly woman:

> [11] The heart of her husband doth safely trust in her, so that he shall have no need of spoil.
> [12] She will do him good and not evil all the days of her life.

This woman's husband has absolute trust in her so that he has no need of satisfaction from other women. She does him good, not evil. And not just every once in a while, but all the days of her life.

> [13] She seeketh wool, and flax, and worketh willingly with her hands.
> [14] She is like the merchants' ships; she bringeth her food from afar.
> [15] She riseth also while it is yet night, and giveth meat to her household, and a portion to her maidens.

She willingly works at home, providing nutritious and tasty food for her family. She gets up in the morning to see that her family is properly fed.

Often these verses are used to describe good businesswomen who—like many tribal women—garden; buy and sell cotton, wool, or flax; weave materials; and sell and distribute what they have made. The role of a woman is varied worldwide, yet these verses seem to include all lifestyles, making it possible for each woman to be considered godly if her work is done with the proper attitude.

She Has Good Business Sense

In Proverbs 31:16–18 we learn that:

> [16] She considereth a field, and buyeth it: with the fruit of her hands she planteth a vineyard.
> [17] She girdeth her loins with strength, and strengtheneth her arms.
> [18] She perceiveth that her merchandise is good: her candle goeth not out by night.

This woman knows a bargain when she sees one. She takes pride in doing a job well, even if she has to stay up late to finish. The strength of her character is seen in her attitude of concern about the future stability of her home.

She Is a Capable Woman

Proverbs 31:19–24 tells us:

> [19] She layeth her hands to the spindle, and her hands
> hold the distaff.
> [20] She stretcheth out her hand to the poor; yea, she
> reacheth forth her hands to the needy.
> [21] She is not afraid of the snow for her household: for
> all her household are clothed with scarlet.
> [22] She maketh herself coverings of tapestry; her cloth-
> ing is silk and purple.
> [23] Her husband is known in the gates, when he sitteth
> among the elders of the land.
> [24] She maketh fine linen, and selleth it; and delivereth
> girdles unto the merchant.

She knows how to make clothing for her family. She cares
about the needy around her. Not only does her family benefit
from her domestic talents, her own clothes show taste and dignity. She is willing to use her abilities to provide extra income.

She Is a Woman of Good Character

We are told about her exceptional character and qualities in
Proverbs 31:25–31:

> [25] Strength and honour are her clothing; and she shall
> rejoice in time to come.

A word picture describes this woman as being clothed with
strength and dignity. Because she has prepared well, she has no
fear about the future; she is full of inner joy and peace.

> [26] She openeth her mouth with wisdom; and in her
> tongue is the law of kindness.
> [27] She looketh well to the ways of her household,
> and eateth not the bread of idleness.
> [28] Her children arise up, and call her blessed; her
> husband also, and he praiseth her.

The godly woman is careful with her tongue. She doesn't gossip, but speaks kind words. Her own children are happy to talk about her to their friends, and her husband brags about her to his friends.

> [29] Many daughters have done virtuously, but thou excellest them all.

This indicates that there are women in the world who do great deeds, but the woman described in these verses ranks highest in God's eyes.

The key to the entire passage is found in verses 30 and 31:

> [30] Favour is deceitful, and beauty is vain: but a woman that feareth the LORD, she shall be praised.
> [31] Give her of the fruit of her hands; and let her own works praise her in the gates.

These verses are like a mirror in which each of us can examine ourselves. Few of us will find our lives reflected here. But we will see the woman we strive to be like, a woman with beauty of spirit and serenity of soul.

CLOSING THOUGHTS

If you were to peer into the mirror of Proverbs 31, what would your image look like? The only way we can be truly godly women is to know the only true God and Jesus Christ, whom He sent to be our Savior. God's love did not stop short of giving His very best to us. He gave His only Son that we should not perish but have eternal life. Jesus loves us so much that He gave His life on the Cross for our sin. Not only did He die, but God raised Him from the dead. Because He lives, you can have eternal life also. If you want the joy and peace that He alone offers, confess your sin, believe in Him, and receive Him as your Savior.

Perhaps you already have trusted in Jesus Christ. If so, I would say to you that the secret of being a godly woman lies in a growing relationship with the Lord Jesus Christ. A woman who knows and loves Him will be praised—perhaps not praised by the world, but praised by God.

I pray you will be grateful to God for the way His Word speaks to women. We are important to Him. God will take what we give to Him—our time, our money, and our skills—and bless us for it.

Before closing this book, let us renew our dedication to God. As Romans 12:1 tells us: let us present our lives to the Lord as a living sacrifice. Having done this, we can trust Him to bless us and to use us for His glory.

FOR DISCUSSION

1. Why is it hard to find a virtuous woman?
2. In what ways does the Bible say she serves her family?
3. Is it wrong for a woman to earn money?
4. What character qualities are listed in this chapter?
5. In what way is a woman's relationship with the Lord her true beauty or lack of it?

BIBLIOGRAPHY

Christensen, Winnie. *Women Who Believed God.* Wheaton, Illinois: Harold Shaw, 1983.

Christensen, Winnie. *Women Who Achieved for God.* Wheaton, Illinois: Harold Shaw, 1984.

Deen, Edith. *All of the Women of the Bible.* New York, New York: Harper & Row, 1955.

Lockyer, Herbert. *All the Women of the Bible.* Grand Rapids, Michigan: Zondervan, 1967.

Matheson, George. *The Representative Women of the Bible.* New York, New York: George H. Doran, 1907.

Smith, Joyce Marie. *A Woman's Priorities.* Wheaton, Illinois: Tyndale House, 1984.

ALPHABETICAL INDEX

NAME	PAGE	NAME	PAGE
Abigail	117	Mary Magdalene	267
Achsah	69	Mary, Martha's Sister	251
Anna	217	Michal	111
Bathsheba	123	Miriam	55
Deborah	75	Naaman's Slave Girl	165
Delilah	81	Naomi	87
Dinah	49	Pharaoh's Daughter	61
Dorcas	277	Priscilla	295
Elizabeth	211	Queen of Sheba	135
Esther	181, 187	Rahab	65
Eunice	301	Rebekah	37
Eve	7	Rhoda	283
Godly Woman	1, 305	Ruth	93, 99
Hagar	25	Salome	221
Hannah	105	Samaritan Woman	257
Harlot Mothers	129	Sapphira	271
Huldah	175	Sarah	13, 19
Jehosheba	169	Shunammite Woman	159
Jezebel	141	Syrophoenician Woman	233
Job's Wife	193	Widow: Oil Multiplied	153
Leah	43	Woman Called "A Sinner"	239
Lot's Wife	31	Woman: Issue of Blood	227
Lydia	289	Woman Taken in Adultery	261
Martha	245	Zarephath Widow	147
Mary, Mother of Jesus	199, 205		

CHRONOLOGICAL INDEX

OLD TESTAMENT

NAME	REFERENCE	PAGE
Eve	Genesis 2	7
Sarah	Genesis 16, 17	13, 19
Hagar	Genesis 16, 17	25
Lot's Wife	Genesis 19	31
Rebekah	Genesis 21	37
Leah	Genesis 29	43
Dinah	Genesis 34	49
Miriam	Exodus 2	55
Pharaoh's Daughter	Exodus 2	61
Rahab	Joshua 2	65
Achsah	Joshua 15	69
Deborah	Judges 4	75
Delilah	Judges 16	81
Naomi	Ruth	87
Ruth	Ruth	93, 99
Hannah	1 Samuel 1	105
Michal	1 Samuel 18	111
Abigail	1 Samuel 25	117
Bathsheba	2 Samuel 11	123
Two Harlot Mothers	1 Kings 3	129
Queen of Sheba	1 Kings 10	135
Jezebel	1 Kings 16	141
Zarephath Widow	1 Kings 17	147
Widow: Oil Multiplied	2 Kings 4	153
Shunammite Woman	2 Kings 4	159
Naaman's Slave Girl	2 Kings 5	165
Jehosheba	2 Kings 11	169

316

NAME	REFERENCE	PAGE
Huldah	2 Kings 22	175
Esther	Esther	181, 187
Job's Wife	Job	193
Godly Woman	Proverbs 31	1, 305

NEW TESTAMENT

NAME	REFERENCE	PAGE
Mary, Mother of Jesus	Matthew 1, 2; Luke 1, 2	199, 205
Elizabeth	Luke 1	211
Anna	Luke 2	217
Salome	Matthew 20	221
Woman: Issue of Blood	Mark 5	227
Syrophoenician	Mark 7	233
Woman Called a "Sinner"	Luke 7	239
Martha	Luke 10	245
Mary, Martha's Sister	Luke 10	251
Samaritan Woman	John 4	257
Woman Taken in Adultery	John 8	261
Mary Magdalene	John 20	267
Sapphira	Acts 5	271
Dorcas	Acts 9	277
Rhoda	Acts 12	283
Lydia	Acts 16	289
Priscilla	Acts 18	295
Eunice	Timothy 2	301